I0812725

IMAGES
of America

LAKE QUINSIGAMOND AND WHITE CITY AMUSEMENT PARK

IMAGES
of America

Lake Quinsigamond and White City Amusement Park

Michael Perna Jr.

ARCADIA
PUBLISHING

ISBN 978-0-7385-3673-6

Published by Arcadia Publishing
Charleston, South Carolina

Printed in the United States of America

Library of Congress Catalog Card Number: 2004108613

For all general information, contact Arcadia Publishing:
Telephone 843-853-2070
Fax 843-853-0044
E-mail sales@arcadiapublishing.com
For customer service and orders:
Toll-free 1-888-313-2665

Visit us on the Internet at www.arcadiapublishing.com

To my loving family.

Contents

INTRODUCTION

White City Amusement Park—even today, mention of this name will evoke an immediate reaction from anyone old enough to remember going to the park. From the day it opened in 1905 until its closing in 1960, the park was a wonderland for young and old alike. People traveled from all over to experience the fun and thrills the park had to offer. The excitement of White City was unmatched anywhere in the area. At first, people would come by foot, by wagon, or on the trolleys from Worcester. The trolleys would carry the throngs of fun-seekers from throughout New England. When the era of the trolley passed, automobiles took over, with families flocking to White City for a summer day's fun. It was only in the years after World War II that the park's luster began to fade. Despite efforts to revitalize the operation, the great White City Park would close on Labor Day 1960, the victim of mismanagement by owners.

White City was the crown jewel in a whole area filled with recreation spots. Development of Lake Quinsigamond as a resort area had begun with the first college regattas held there in the late 1850s. Despite interruption during the Civil War years, the lake was rapidly turned into one huge pleasure resort. Throughout the latter part of the 19th century and well into the 20th century, Lake Quinsigamond's shores were packed with social, ethnic, and athletic clubs, summer hotels, and boat and canoe rental businesses. In addition to White City and the older Lincoln Park on the Worcester shore, there were picnic grounds, a horse-racing track, a bicycle- and motorcycle-racing track, an antique car museum, boys' and girls' camps, many dance halls, nightclubs, restaurants, and innumerable summer cottages. All in all, quite a fun place to visit!

In the latter part of the 20th century, slowly one club after another was sold off or burned. The amusement parks closed, and summer cottages were upgraded to year-round homes; the old lake was changing forever. Today, very little remains of what was once one of the premier recreation areas in all of New England.

This book, *Lake Quinsigamond and White City Amusement Park*, will allow readers to revisit the glory days of the old lake. Old photographs and postcards bring back images of exactly what existed in years past—all the excitement and fun that once could be found at the lake.

Of course, as years go by, these old photos and postcards become more and more rare. I must acknowledge the help of several individuals who were kind enough to lend just such items from their personal collections to allow this work to be completed. They include Barton Kamp of Worcester, Massachusetts; Erik Larson of Southbridge, Massachusetts; John Richardson and

Paul DiCicco of Millbury, Massachusetts; and the Krafve and Garganigo families, of Northborough and Shrewsbury, Massachusetts, respectively. I would also be remiss if I failed to recognize my entire family, who have once again somehow tolerated my constant burrowing through old papers and records, postcards, and photographs, and long hours spent working on this book. In addition, I would like to thank Michael Paika of Shrewsbury for his constant, infectious enthusiasm and encouragement. Without all of these people, and many others who have helped along the way, this particular documentation of an important part of our local history would not have been possible. Thank you one and all.

—Michael Perna Jr., Shrewsbury, Massachusetts, July 2004.

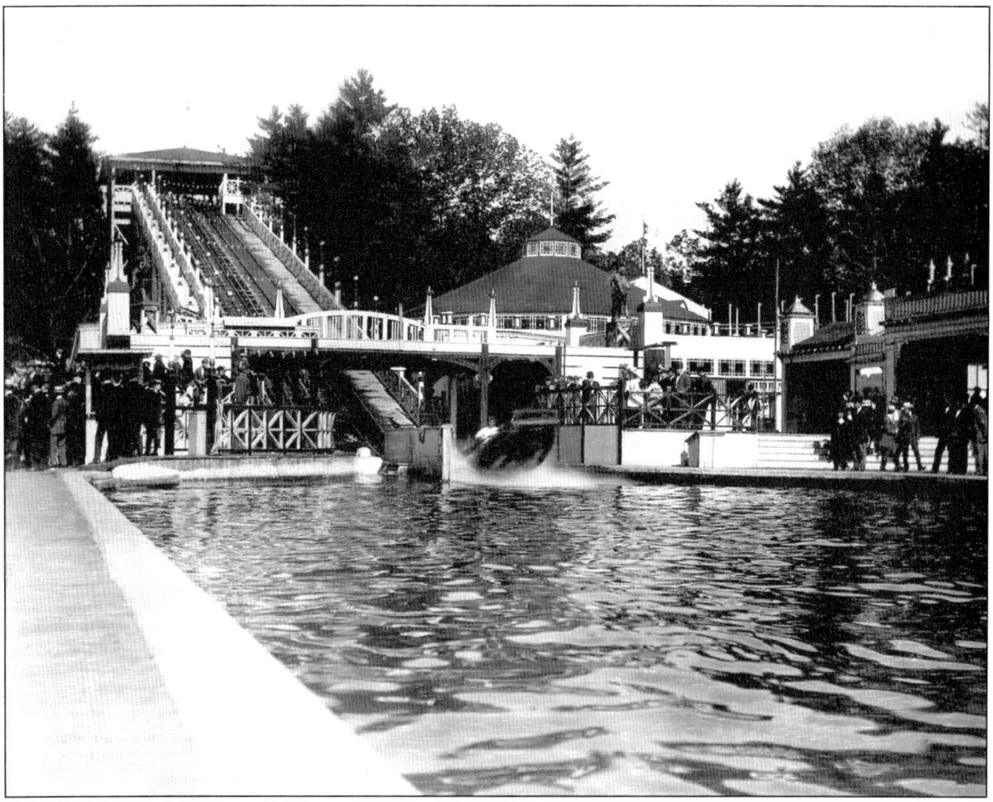

The great White City Amusement Park opened in 1905. It was closed in 1955 after entertaining and thrilling innumerable thousands of people. The Shoot the Chutes ride pictured here was the main attraction at the park from the time it opened until a major renovation in the late 1920s. Today, many modern amusement parks feature rides that are very similar to the Shoot the Chutes.

One

Lincoln Park, the Causeway, and Crew Racing

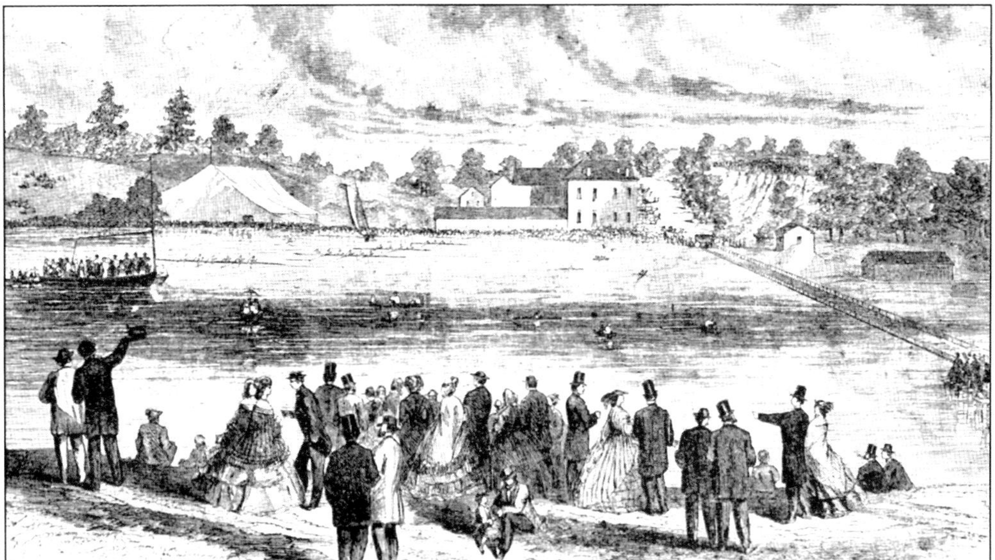

One of the earliest Lake Quinsigamond scenes is this woodcut entitled "Lake Quinsigamond in the Regatta Days of Auld Lang Syne – View from near Regatta Point." The Pond Tavern House is seen to the left of the floating bridge. The spectators are standing roughly where Regatta Point State Park is today. The Pond Tavern House itself was not well regarded in the town of Shrewsbury. After the building burned to the ground, one resident recorded the event in his diary with words to the effect that the town and its people would not be greatly troubled by the loss of the place. Judging from earlier diary entries, it would appear that the Pond Tavern House was a source of drinking and mayhem. The small structure to the right of the floating bridge was Dr. John Green's boathouse. The well-known Worcester doctor was the first person to cross the bridge when it was built.

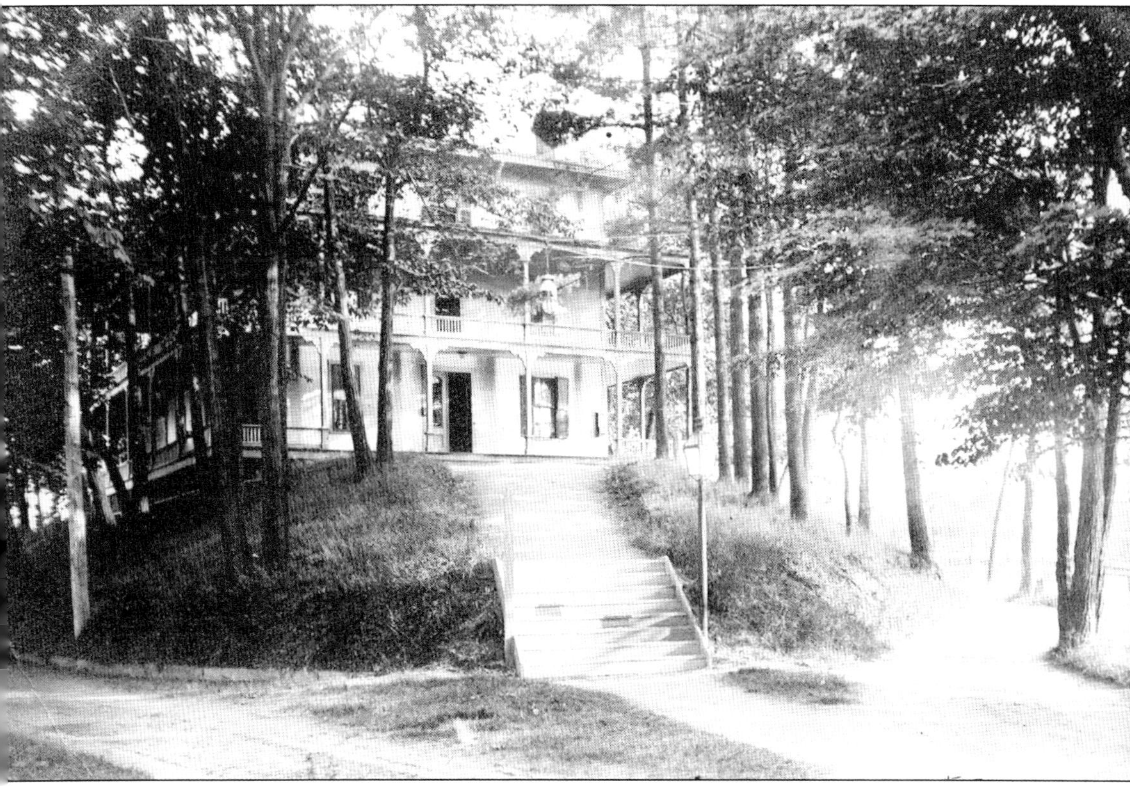

The Quinsigamond House Hotel was built by Jesse Johnson (J. J.) Coburn, who had returned to the area from the Gold Rush of 1849. The construction of the Quinsigamond House was the first step in the huge development of the Lake Quinsigamond area that followed in later years. The hotel was later known as the Island House, Belmont House, and Thule Club. It was torn down after the Route 9 bridge was completed. The raised area where the hotel building once stood is still obvious to passers-by today. (Courtesy Erik Larson.)

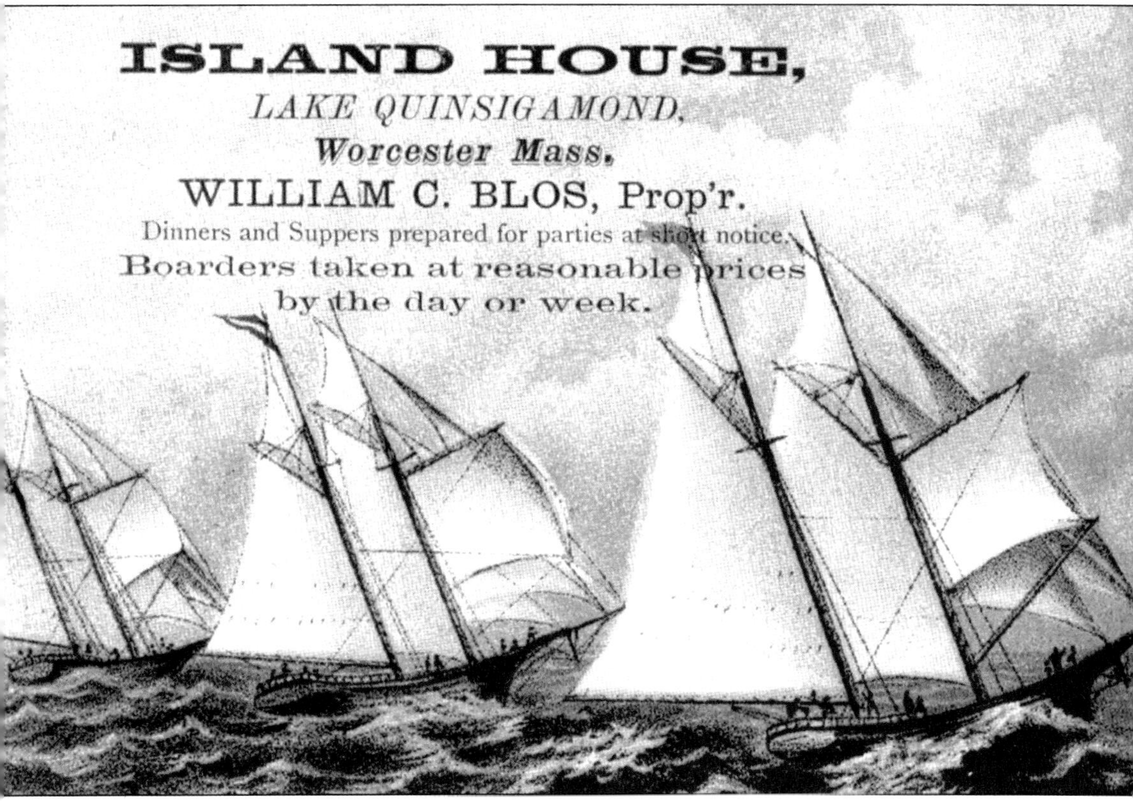

This scene was one among a whole series that were produced on cards advertising the Island House. All of the cards featured scenes with a nautical theme, none of which had any direct connection to the actual location of the hotel on Lake Quinsigamond.

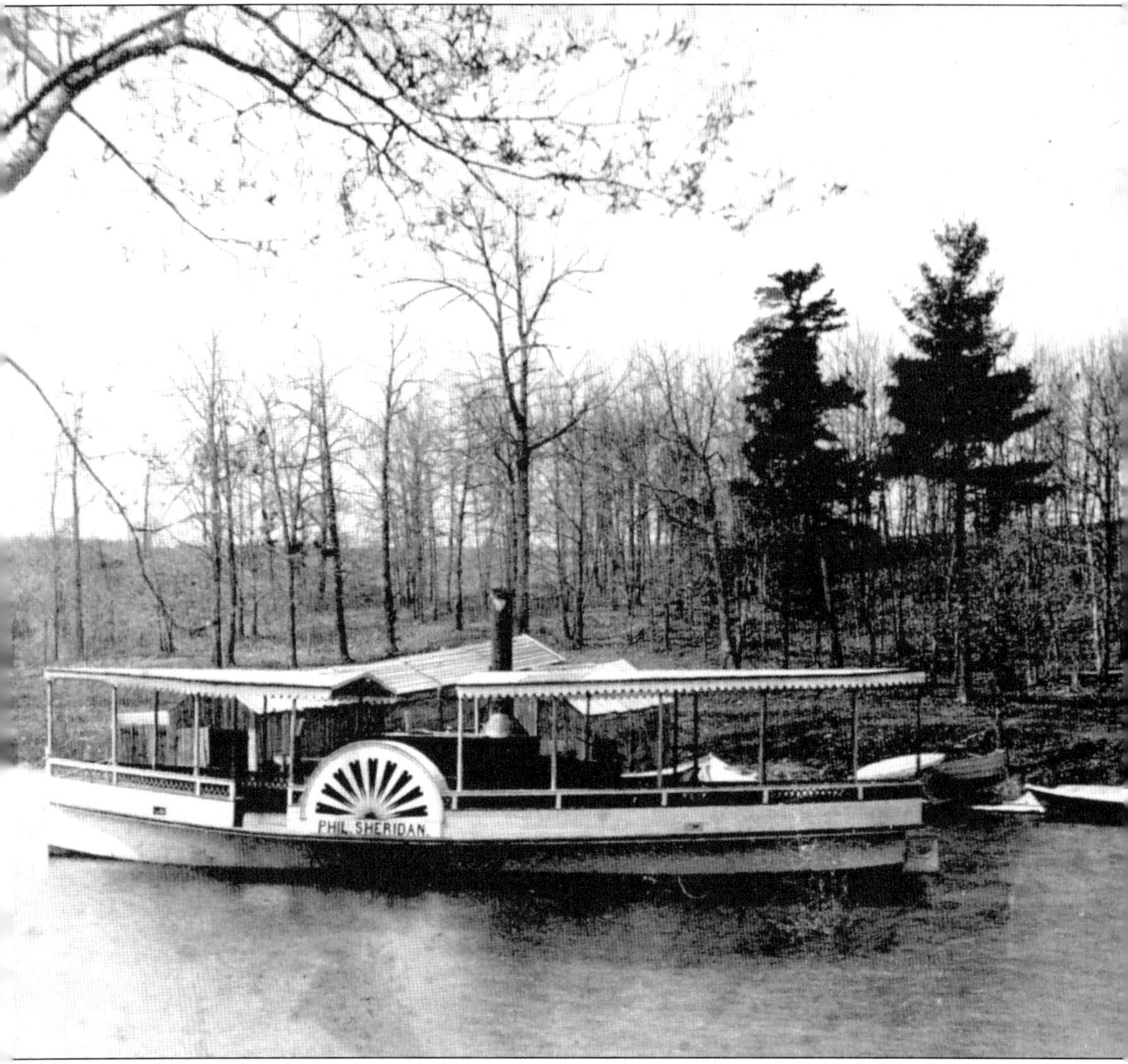

Although a steamboat operated on Lake Quinsigamond as early as 1847, it wasn't until J. J. Coburn built the *Phil Sheridan* and put it into service just after the Civil War that the idea caught on. This boat was quickly followed by others; the *Addie* and *Little Favorite* were in operation by 1873. The number of steamboats grew until all shapes and sizes were sailing on the lake, with landings up and down its shores. Such steamboats included the *Zephyr*, *Tatassit*, *Meteor*, *Venus*, *Apollo*, *Dewey*, *Dauntless*, *Uncle Sam*, and *Colonel Isaac Davis*. Other smaller versions, known as steam launches, were also prevalent on the lake. By the late 1920s, almost all of the steamboats were gone, replaced by more modern gasoline-powered craft. The side-wheeler *Phil Sheridan* is shown in this 1868 photograph.

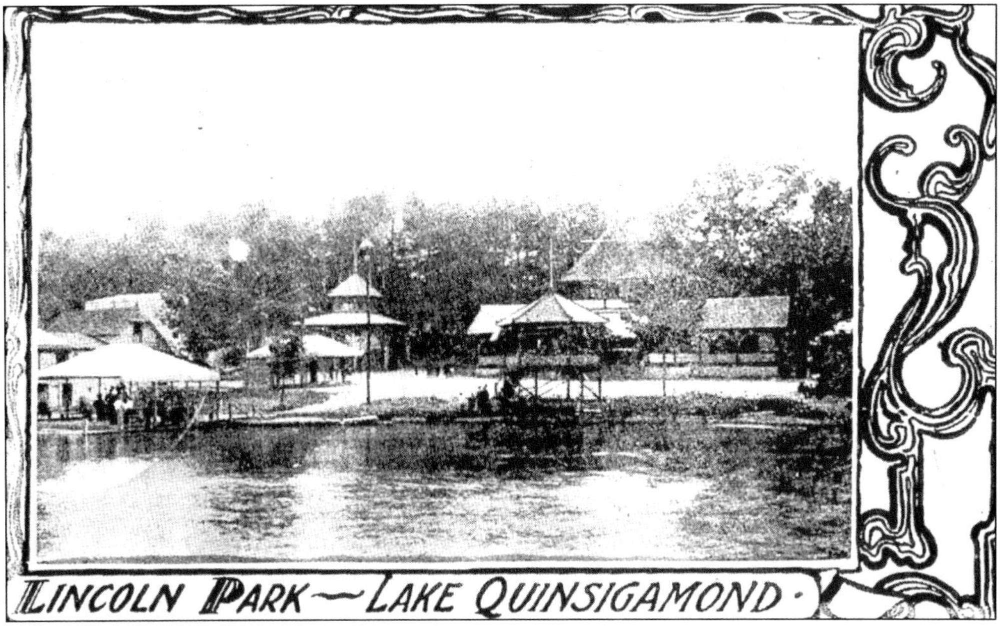

This is a rare metallic postcard, imprinted with a view of Lincoln Park. Similar cards were made showing White City Amusement Park. This particular card was actually mailed to an address in Millbury, Massachusetts, in 1906. We can only wonder at the havoc this metal postcard might play with today's electronic mail-sorting machines. Various types of souvenirs were produced for the amusement parks, most advertising the parks they were sold at. Popular items included ruby red "flash glass" cups, pitchers, toothpick holders, and the like. Most of these souvenirs originated at White City and had "White City" or "White City Worcester, Mass." etched into the glass. Others had the date or owner's name inscribed.

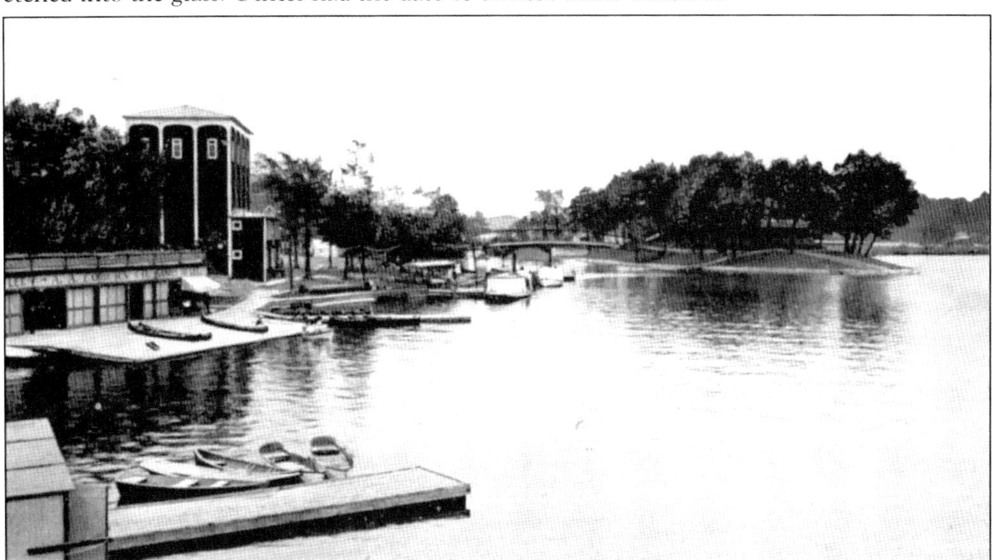

Lincoln Park lined the Worcester shore starting at the causeway, extending to the south for quite a distance. This particular view looks northward toward the park on the left. In the foreground is the A. A. Coburn boathouse and docks, with the Lincoln Park theater (the high building) in the distance to the rear. The small bridge from Thule Island to Lincoln Park is just visible.

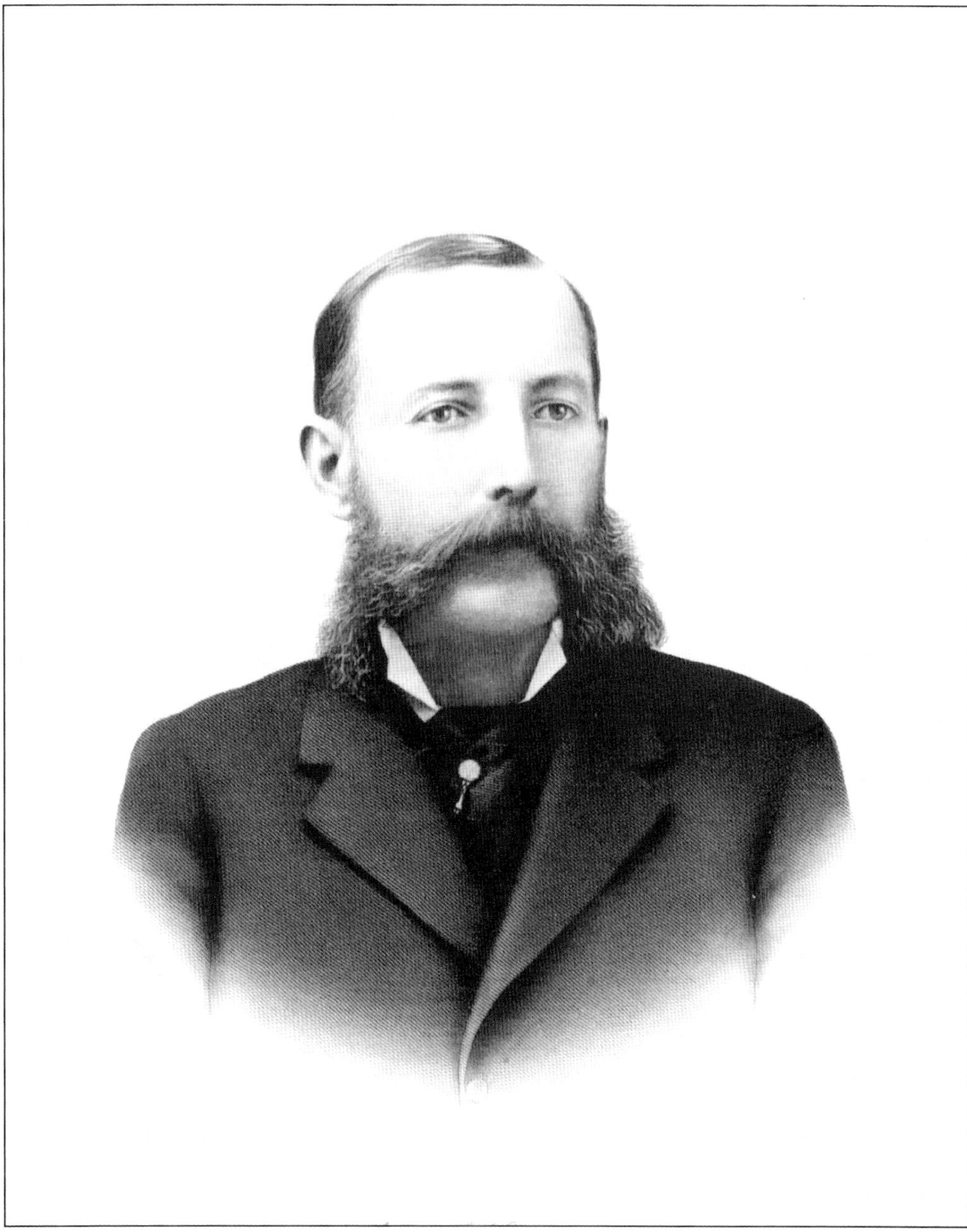

Jesse Johnson (J. J.) Coburn was the first person to begin developing the area around Lake Quinsigamond into a pleasure resort. He started by building the Quinsigamond House Hotel, putting a steamboat into service, and creating an early amusement park, Lincoln Park, on the Worcester shore. Coburn later developed great tracts of land around the lake and the Worcester and Shrewsbury Railroad. Streets in the Lake View area are named after Coburn's family (Coburn Avenue) and his son Alvarado (Alvarado Avenue). One of Coburn's later endeavors was the steamboat *Colonel Isaac Davis*, which was wrecked shortly after being put into service. A number of passengers were killed or injured in the incident. Coburn, who reportedly never got over the tragic event, died a few years later at the age of 53. Many people attributed his death to a broken heart.

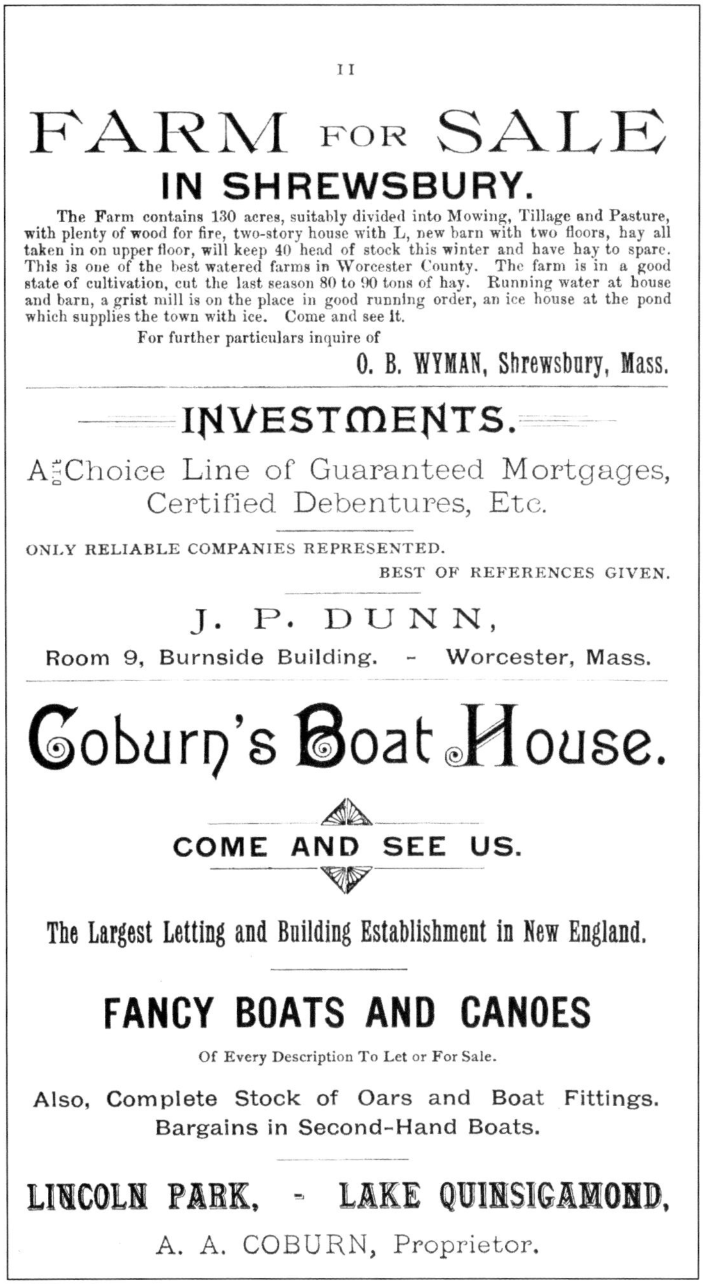
II

FARM FOR SALE
IN SHREWSBURY.

The Farm contains 130 acres, suitably divided into Mowing, Tillage and Pasture, with plenty of wood for fire, two-story house with L, new barn with two floors, hay all taken in on upper floor, will keep 40 head of stock this winter and have hay to spare. This is one of the best watered farms in Worcester County. The farm is in a good state of cultivation, cut the last season 80 to 90 tons of hay. Running water at house and barn, a grist mill is on the place in good running order, an ice house at the pond which supplies the town with ice. Come and see it.

For further particulars inquire of

O. B. WYMAN, Shrewsbury, Mass.

INVESTMENTS.

A Choice Line of Guaranteed Mortgages, Certified Debentures, Etc.

ONLY RELIABLE COMPANIES REPRESENTED.

BEST OF REFERENCES GIVEN.

J. P. DUNN,

Room 9, Burnside Building. - Worcester, Mass.

Coburn's Boat House.

COME AND SEE US.

The Largest Letting and Building Establishment in New England.

FANCY BOATS AND CANOES

Of Every Description To Let or For Sale.

Also, Complete Stock of Oars and Boat Fittings.
Bargains in Second-Hand Boats.

LINCOLN PARK, - LAKE QUINSIGAMOND,

A. A. COBURN, Proprietor.

This advertisement for Coburn's Boat House appeared in an 1890 booklet. Coburn's Boat House stood just south of Lincoln Park on the Worcester shore. Alvarado Alonzo (A. A.) Coburn had taken over his father's business interests at the lake. Coburn's Boat House was in great competition with Robertson's Boat House, and later on, Crandell's Boat House, which stood nearby. A. A. Coburn was very successful and probably would have passed his businesses down to his son, but the young man was killed in a sledding accident. In a weird coincidence, young Coburn was sledding down a hill on Coburn Avenue, where the family had developed the Lake View neighborhood. The site of the boat house was located roughly where a tall condominium complex stands on Lake Avenue today.

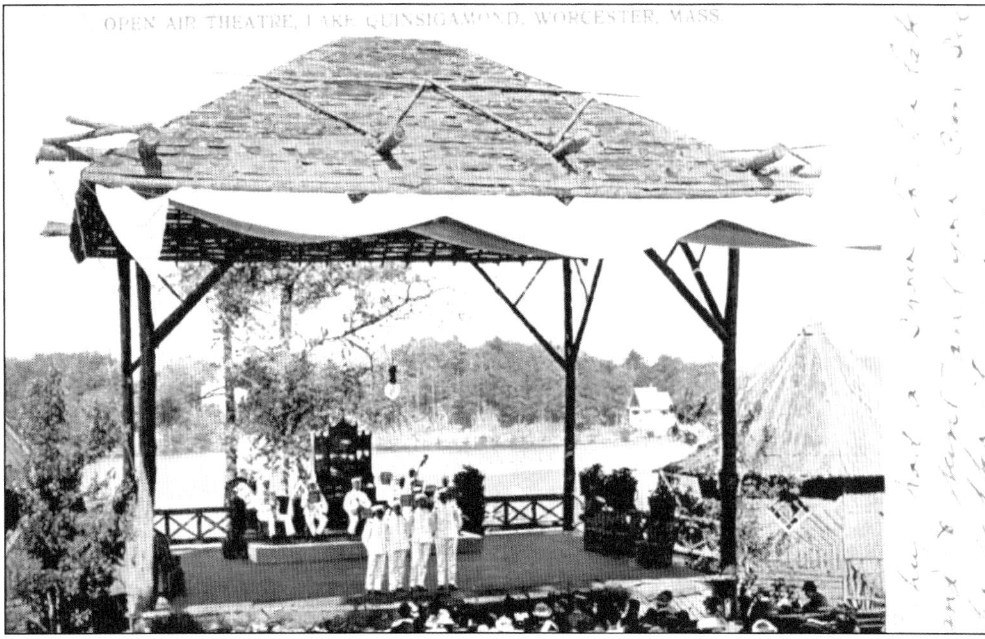

The Open Air Theater, shown here, was constantly in use at Lincoln Park. All types of singing, dancing, and comedy acts appeared on the little stage (to say nothing of the occasional wild animal act). July 31, 1903, was a memorable day for the theater crowd. That evening, a severe downpour struck, driving the audience to seek shelter under the canvas canopy that covered part of the seating area. Unfortunately, the canopy rapidly filled with water, and the whole structure sagged and groaned, threatening to collapse on the people underneath. At this point, police officers Garrett Fitzgerald and Robert Matthews came to the rescue, slicing holes in the canvas to let the water escape.

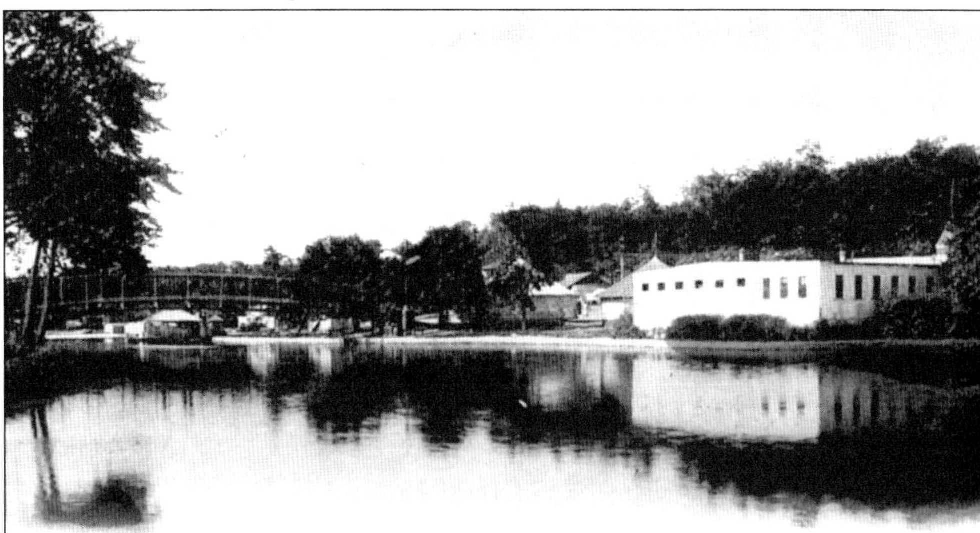

The Lincoln Park dance hall, which later was used as a roller skating rink, is shown here on the right side of this 1905 view looking southward from the causeway. The dance hall was one of the last remnants of Lincoln Park. The hall even served as the venue for a number of sock hops held in an attempt to bring the park back to life, before the building was destroyed by fire in the 1960s.

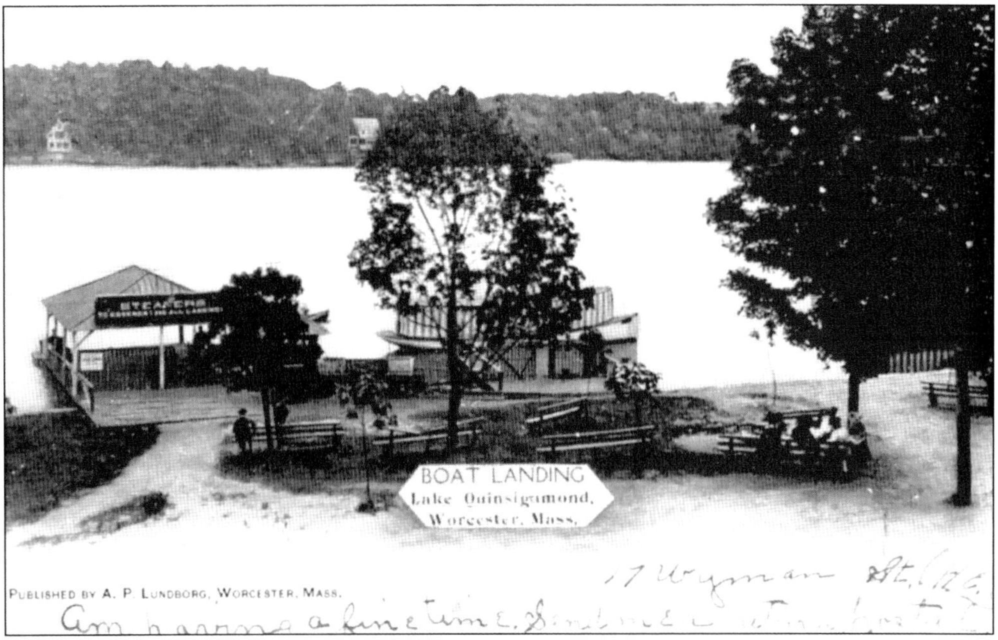

This early view of the Lincoln Park boat landing shows one of the steamers at anchor with what appear to be curtains drawn around the boat's seating area. The sign at the little dock reads, "To Edgemere and all Landings." This particular card is dated 1902, three years before the great White City Park opened across the lake.

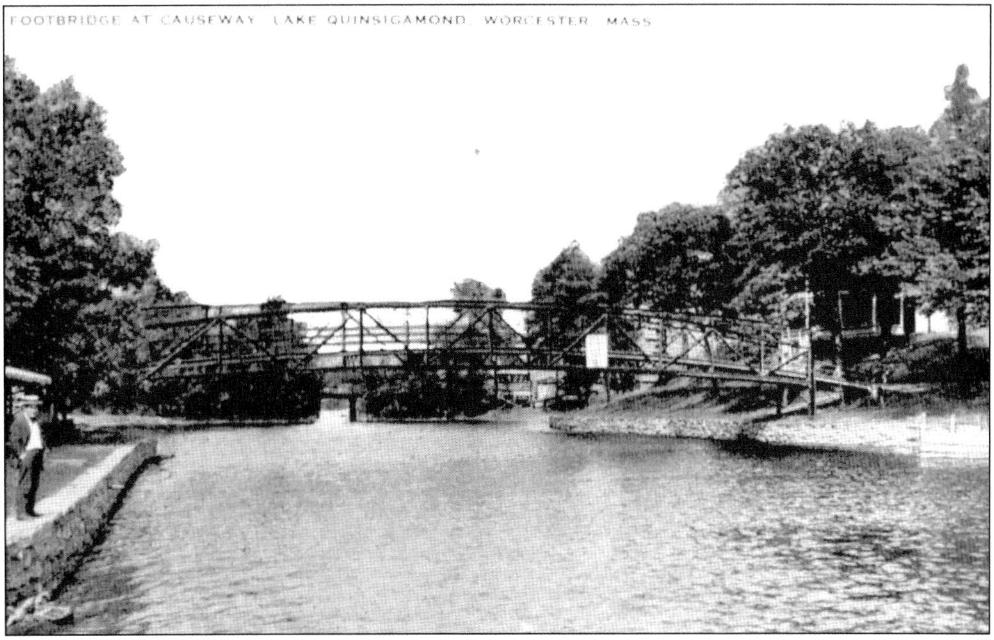

Spanning the lake from Lincoln Park to Thule Island, this little bridge allowed people a much shorter route between the amusement park and summer hotel. Originally built of wood, the later version shown here was made of metal. The bridge fell into disrepair and eventually was blocked off to pedestrians. This didn't stop young boys from squeezing through the blocked entrances to sit on the bridge and fish, however. The bridge was ultimately torn down.

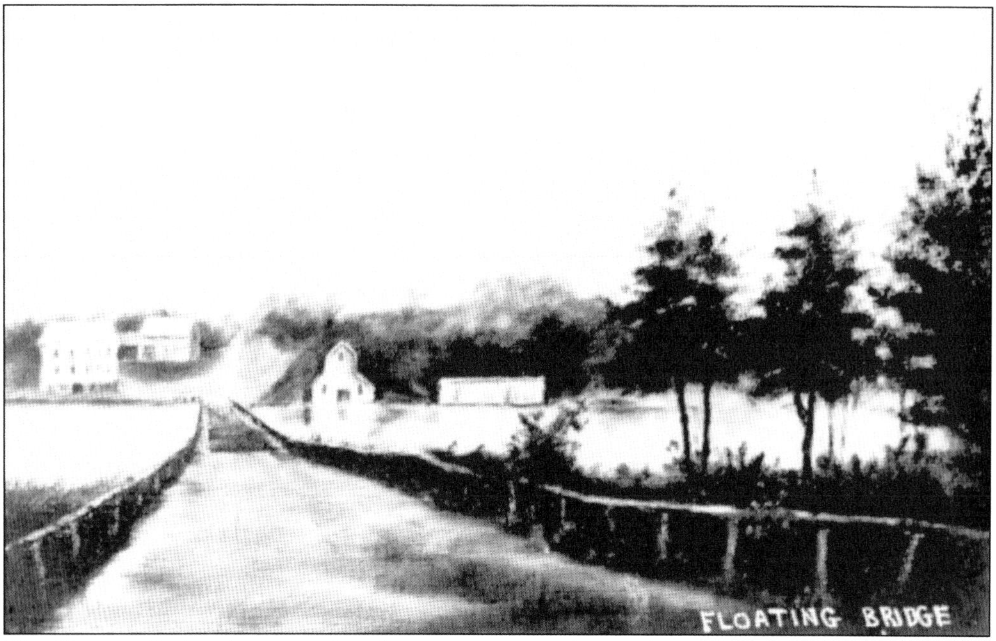

The Floating Bridge shown in this drawing was one of a number that spanned the lake at the same point as the current Route 9 bridge. The floating bridges would roll and sway when carriages passed over them, sometimes sinking low enough that the wheels of the carriage would get wet. The floating bridges were used until the causeway was put in place in the early 1860s.

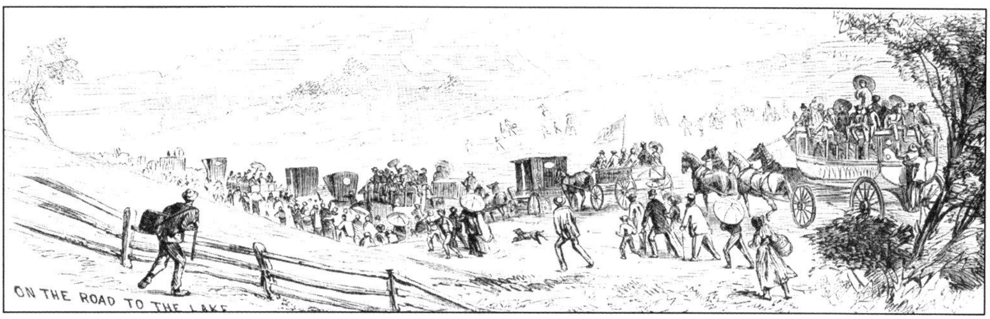

Entitled *On the Road to the Lake*, this woodcut was described as "a spirited sketch, showing how the scene of the contest was reached amidst the most delightful confusion." These people were hurrying toward Lake Quinsigamond for the college regatta held on July 19, 1867. Carriages and wagons can be seen traveling westward in the area that is now occupied by shopping centers and businesses of all types. Lake Quinsigamond is just out of view to the left.

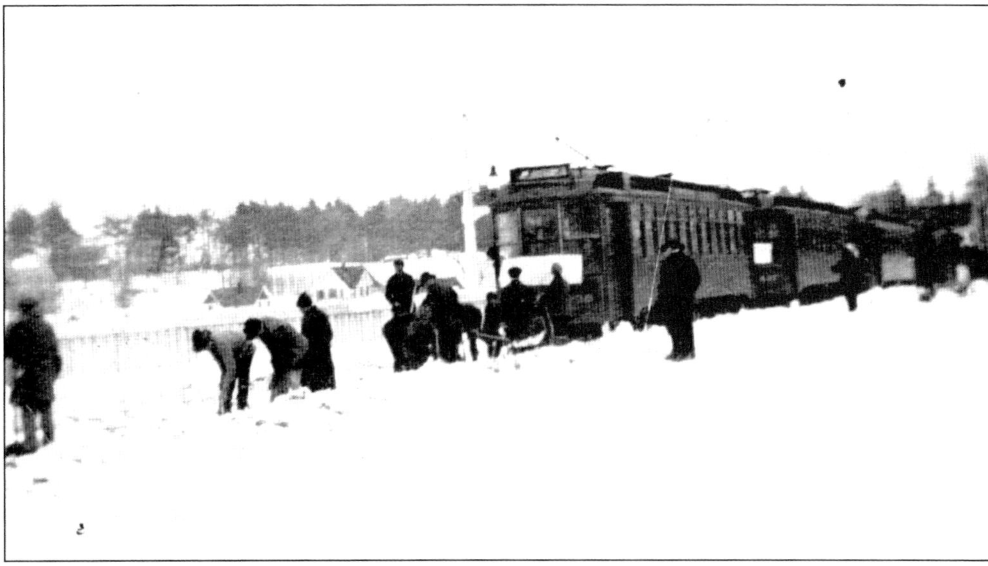

During the first week of February 1920, a great snowstorm brought the Worcester area to a standstill. Businesses were closed, milk deliveries were halted, and at least two trolleys (one in Marlborough and one in Westborough) were abandoned on the tracks. The snow was so deep that the trolleys were not found until the following week. Shown here is a group of men trying to clear the trolley tracks on the Lake Quinsigamond Bridge in order to let the trolleys pass over into Worcester.

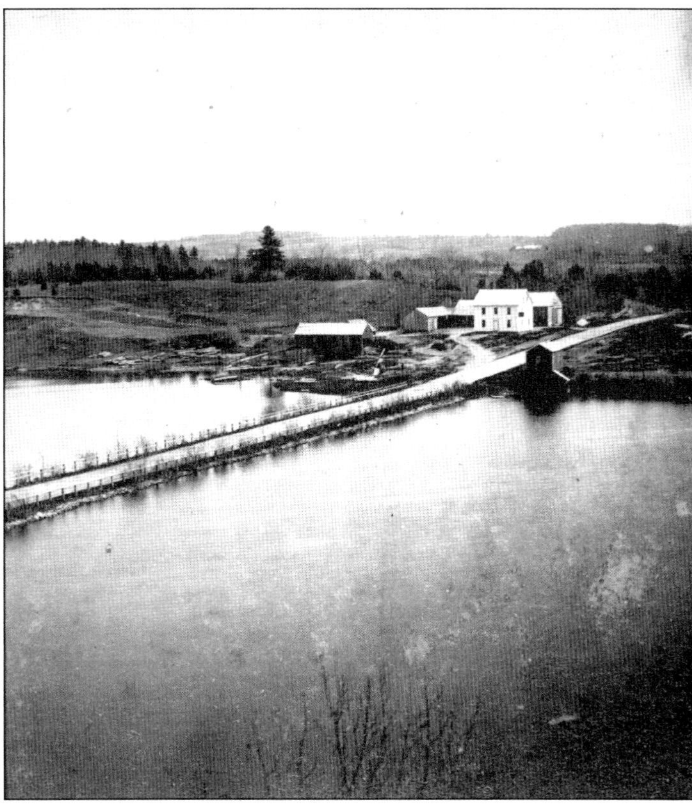

This view may represent one of the earliest known photographs of Lake Quinsigamond. The picture can be approximately dated to 1862, as the causeway was finished and the Pond Tavern House (seen on the Shrewsbury shore) burned the same year. Judging from the high elevation, it is likely that the photograph was taken during a balloon ascension at the lake.

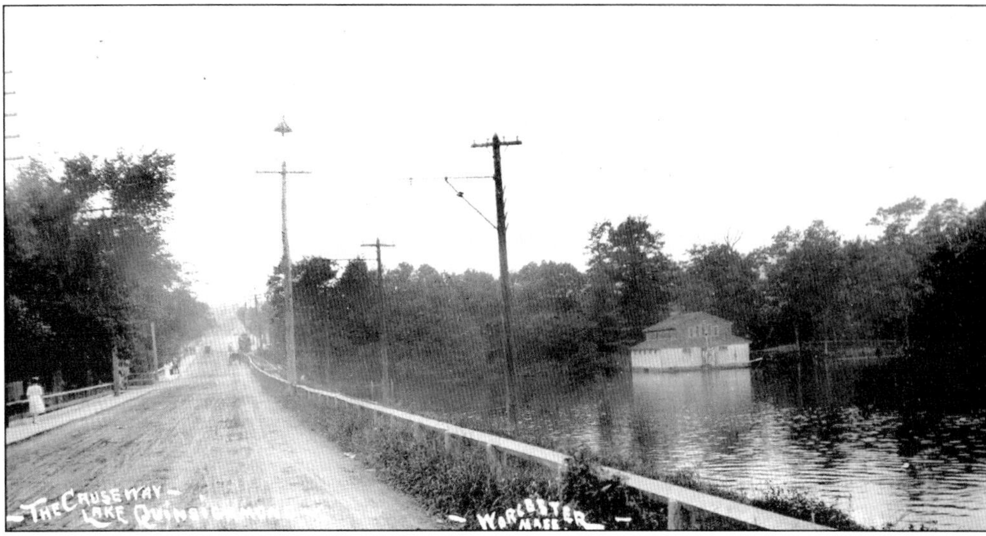

This is a view of the causeway, looking westward toward Belmont Street in Worcester. This photograph is unusual in that almost every other similar shot is taken looking eastward, into Shrewsbury. The Women's Bath House at what is now Regatta Point can be seen in the distance to the right. (Courtesy Barton Kamp.)

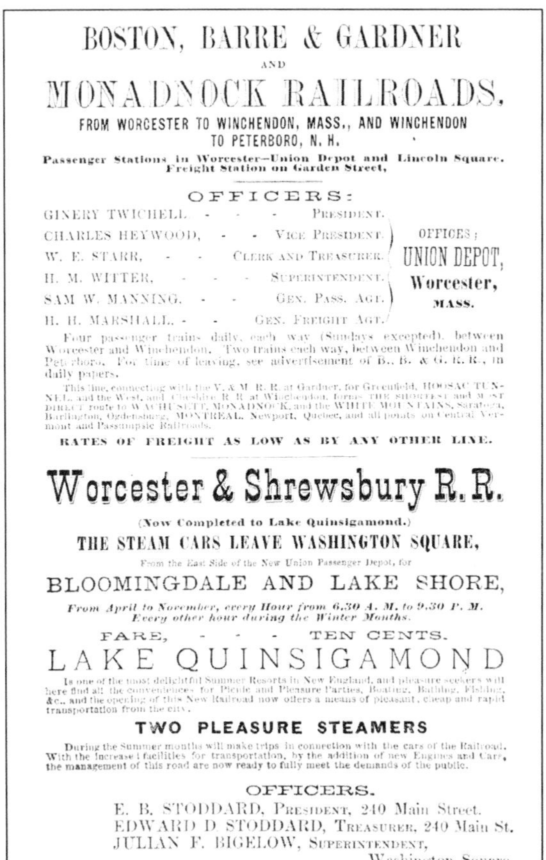

BOSTON, BARRE & GARDNER

AND

MONADNOCK RAILROADS,

FROM WORCESTER TO WINCHENDON, MASS., AND WINCHENDON TO PETERBORO, N. H.

Passenger Stations in Worcester—Union Depot and Lincoln Square. Freight Station on Garden Street,

OFFICERS:

GINERY TWICHELL, - - - PRESIDENT.
CHARLES HEYWOOD, - - VICE PRESIDENT.
W. E. STARR, - - CLERK AND TREASURER.
H. M. WITTER, - - - SUPERINTENDENT.
SAM W. MANNING, - - GEN. PASS. AGT.
H. H. MARSHALL, - - GEN. FREIGHT AGT.

OFFICES; UNION DEPOT, Worcester, MASS.

Four passenger trains daily, each way (Sundays excepted), between Worcester and Winchendon. Two trains each way, between Winchendon and Peterboro. For time of leaving, see advertisement of B., B. & G. R. R., in daily papers.

This line, connecting with the V. & M. R. R. at Gardner, for Greenfield, HOOSAC TUNNEL, and the West, and Cheshire R. R. at Winchendon, forms THE SHORTEST and MOST DIRECT route to WACHUSETT, MONADNOCK, and the WHITE MOUNTAINS, Saratoga, Burlington, Ogdensburg, MONTREAL, Newport, Quebec, and all points on Central Vermont and Passumpsic Railroads.

RATES OF FREIGHT AS LOW AS BY ANY OTHER LINE.

Worcester & Shrewsbury R. R.

(Now Completed to Lake Quinsigamond.)

THE STEAM CARS LEAVE WASHINGTON SQUARE,

From the East Side of the New Union Passenger Depot, for

BLOOMINGDALE AND LAKE SHORE,

From April to November, every Hour from 6.30 A. M. to 9.30 P. M. Every other hour during the Winter Months.

FARE, - - - TEN CENTS.

LAKE QUINSIGAMOND

Is one of the most delightful Summer Resorts in New England, and pleasure seekers will here find all the conveniences for Picnic and Pleasure Parties, Boating, Bathing, Fishing, &c., and the opening of this New Railroad now offers a means of pleasant, cheap and rapid transportation from the city.

TWO PLEASURE STEAMERS

During the Summer months will make trips in connection with the cars of the Railroad. With the increased facilities for transportation, by the addition of new Engines and Cars, the management of this road are now ready to fully meet the demands of the public.

OFFICERS.

E. B. STODDARD, PRESIDENT, 240 Main Street.
EDWARD D. STODDARD, TREASURER, 240 Main St.
JULIAN F. BIGELOW, SUPERINTENDENT, Washington Square.

The Worcester and Shrewsbury Railroad, sometimes known as the "dummy" railroad, began operation in 1873. It was a narrow-gauge line, running 2.7 miles from Union Station down to the lake. The line was built for the express purpose of bringing paying customers to the attractions at Lake Quinsigamond. The effort was very successful; a report from 1877 claims that the little railroad carried between "110,000 to 115,000" passengers annually.

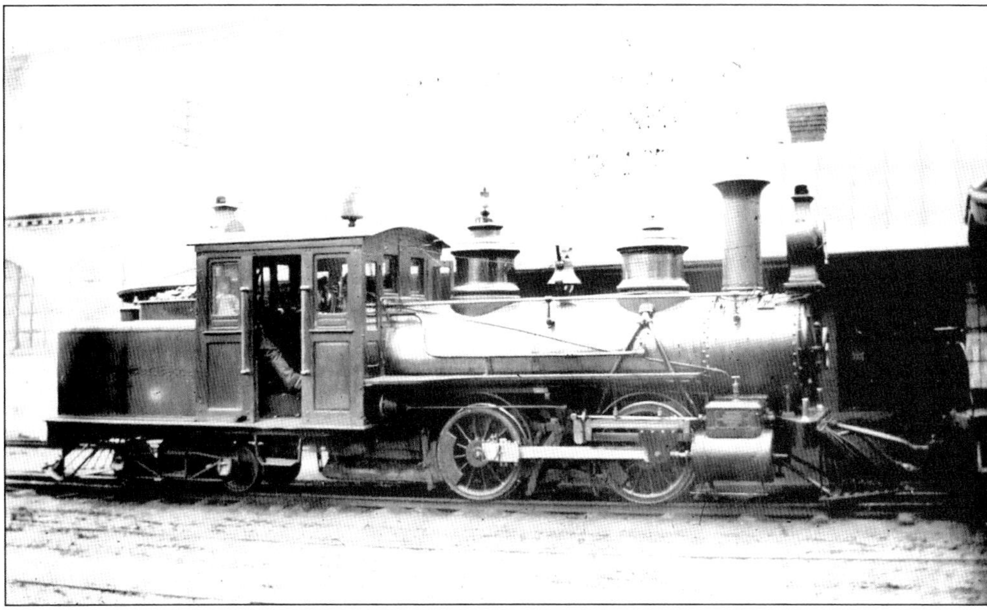

The Worcester and Shrewsbury Railroad added more rolling stock as passenger traffic increased. By 1890, the little railroad had four locomotives and eight passenger cars. At this time, it was making 22 round trips per day in the summer and 18 in the winter, with 4 to 6 extra round trips almost daily. The line's Number 4 locomotive is shown in this photograph. The little railroad was eventually widened to standard gauge, with trolleys replacing the locomotives and passenger cars. Like most of Worcester's trolleys, the Worcester and Shrewsbury Railroad ceased operation in the 1920s.

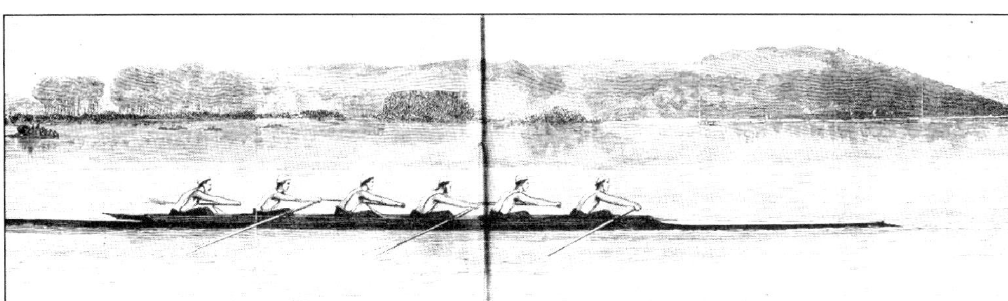

This image depicts the Harvard and Yale crews competing in the college regatta held July 19, 1867. The woodcut print appeared in the *Harper's Weekly* of August 3, 1867. The races were held "after a night of the wildest festivities." The Harvard crew ended up beating Yale by a considerable margin.

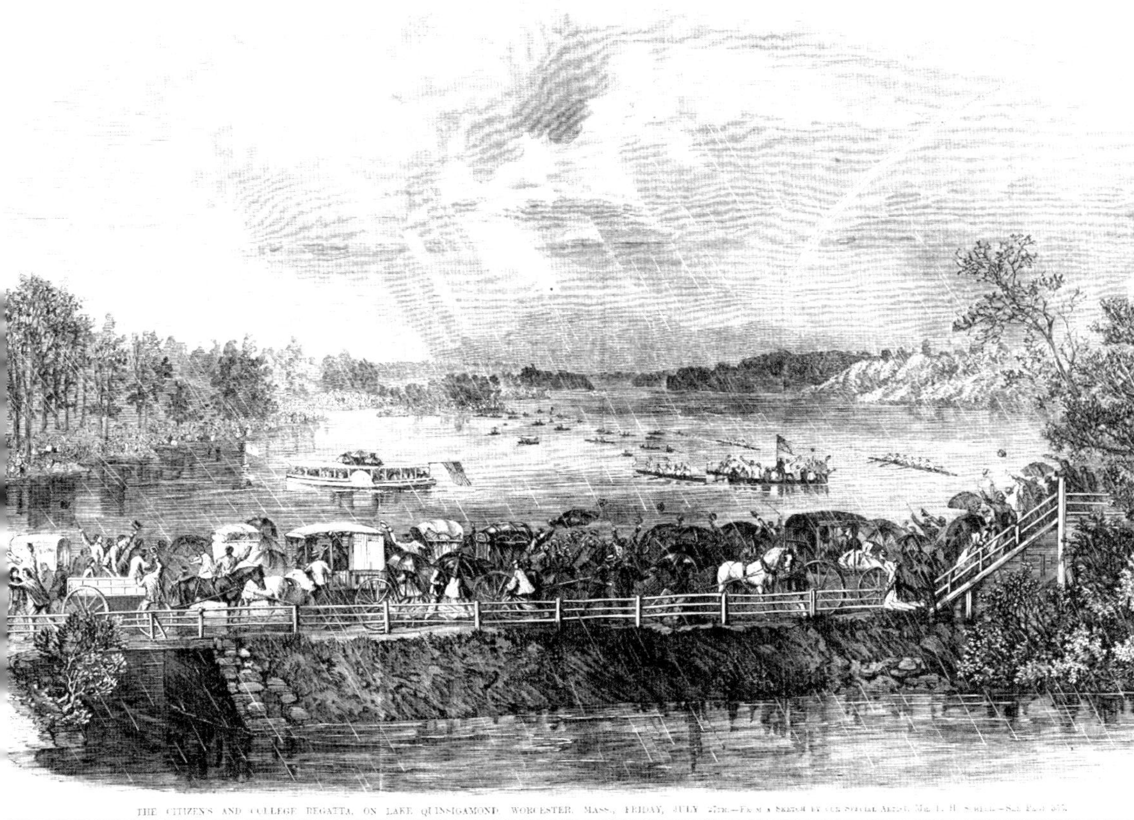

This woodcut print appeared in *Frank Leslie's Illustrated Newspaper* in August 1866. It shows the Citizen's and College Regatta that took place on July 27 of that year. The scene presents a northward view toward the causeway, which is full of carriages and spectators. The racing shells, along with the steamboat *Phil Sheridan*, can be seen in the distance. A very accurate depiction, this view includes the rain showers that dampened race day, and even a rainbow! In the most anticipated race of the day, Harvard beat Yale by a wide margin. Interestingly, regattas are held in this same exact area even today. Several woodcuts of this type, portraying college regattas, appeared in newspapers similar to this one during the 1860s.

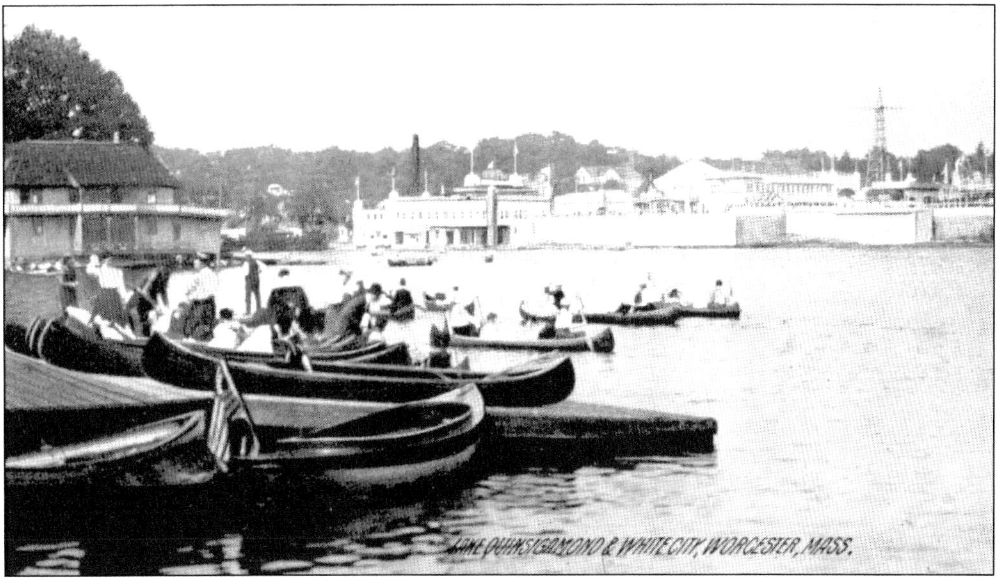

A view looking northeastward from Lincoln Park toward White City. The boathouse building at the south end of Ramshorn Island can be seen to the left, with White City Amusement Park across the lake. This would be a typical scene on any given weekend in the era before motorboats became popular, with large numbers of people renting canoes for a day's outing on the lake. Several old-timers remember that one would need to get down to the lake early on a weekend morning to get a canoe, before they were all rented out.

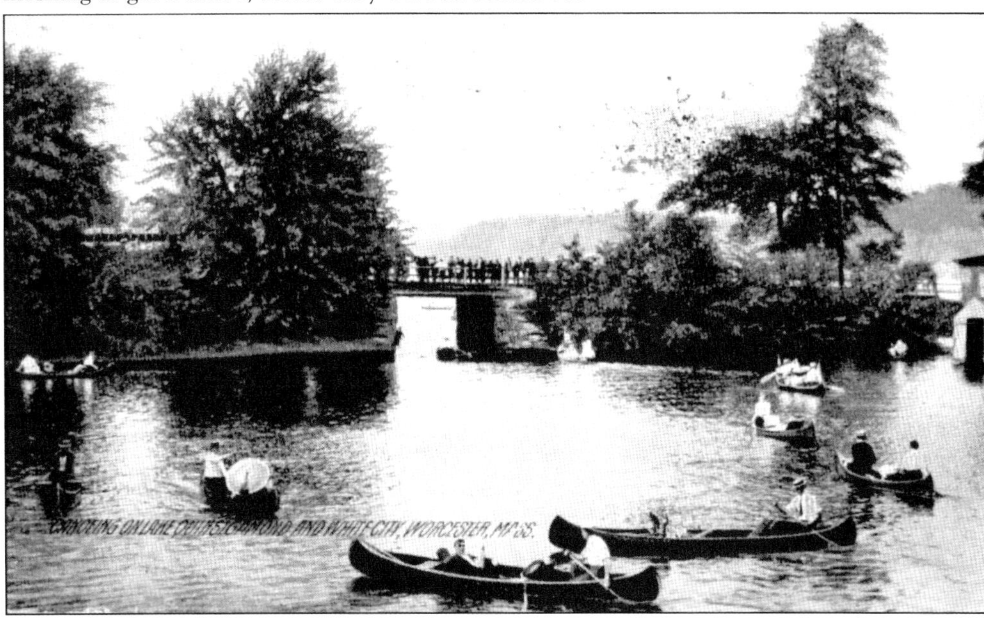

This small opening in the causeway was the only way to pass from the northern to the southern parts of the lake. This was the area where the famous "Ghost of Lake Quinsigamond" was first sighted. The "ghost" was the creation of John Cumming, a well-known rower, who had built the apparition from wire and old sheets. In 1903, people were scared witless by the spooky spirit, which was towed along behind a boat. It was only when shots were fired at the ghost that Cumming decided to own up to being the ghost's creator!

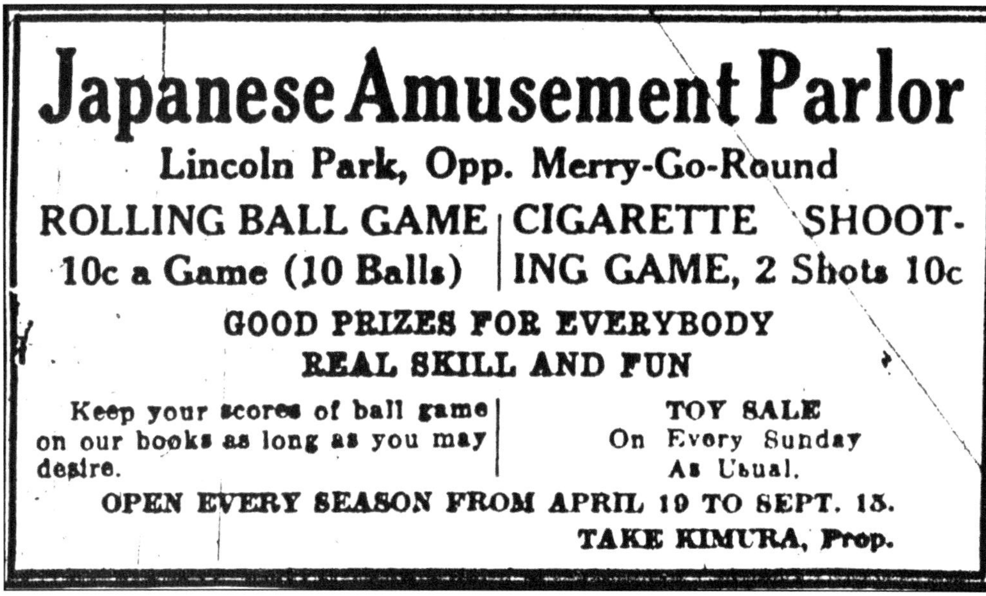

One of the many games of chance at Lincoln Park was run by Take Kimura. The particular game advertised here was described by John Cumming, who grew up near the park, in a 1990s account: "The game was run by Taki Kamur [*sic*]...large, ornate displays of fancy dishes from China and Japan enticed participants to roll rubber balls along a miniature bowling alley in hopes of winning a dish or two. Some came back regularly in an effort to fill out a whole set of dishes." The other half of Kimura's stand held a shooting gallery where people tried to knock over packs of cigarettes.

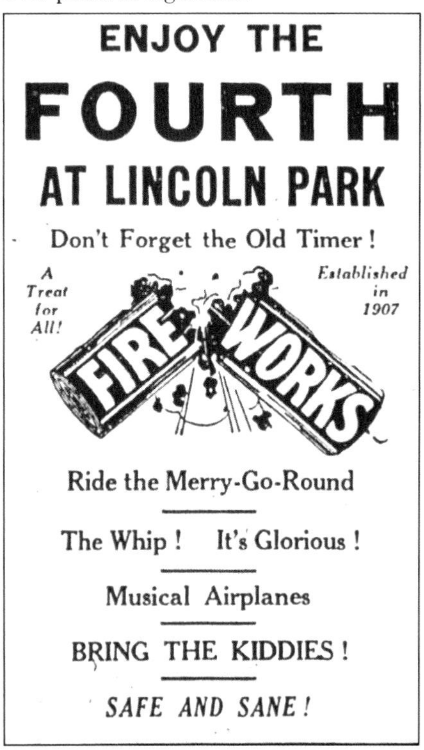

The Fourth of July was *the* big day of the year at the lake. Fireworks displays were held, crackers and rockets of all types were fired, and general mayhem ensued. People would spend the whole night at the lake, not returning home until dawn. Boats and canoes covered the lake's surface, prompting some to tell the story that a person could walk from shore to shore without getting his feet wet. Lake Quinsigamond on the Fourth of July is a much tamer place today.

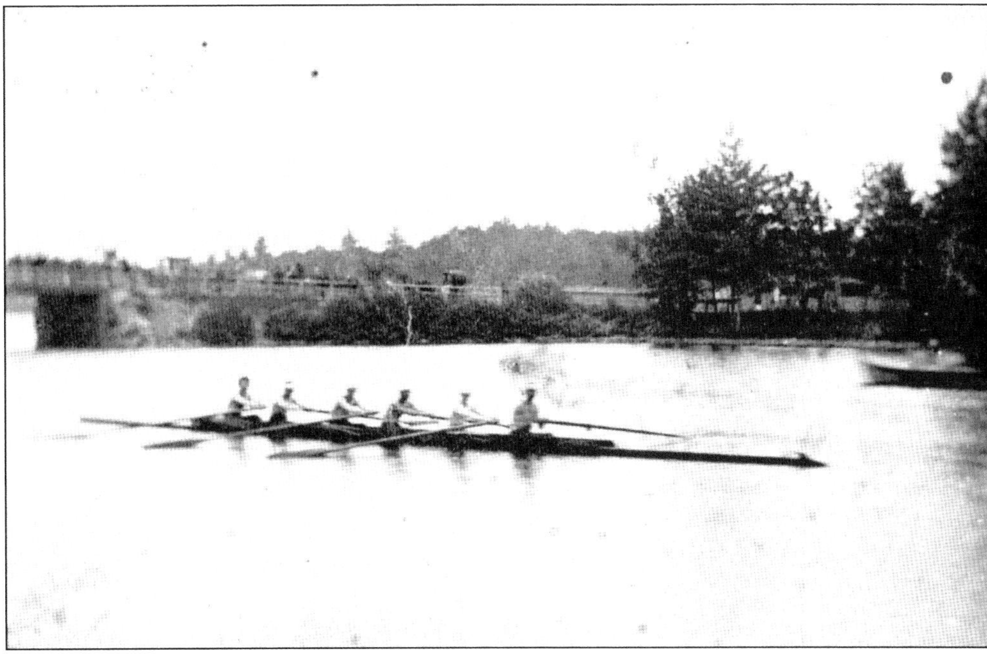

This early regatta photograph shows the Springfield six-oared crew rowing southward toward the opening in the causeway. The rowers from left to right are J. O'Neil (stroke), P. Bryan, F. Parker, Geo. Boyle, J. Boyle, and J. A. Lynch (bow). This was one of a series of stereopticon cards entitled "Views of Lake Quinsigamond" published by L. H. Stockwell, a Worcester optician.

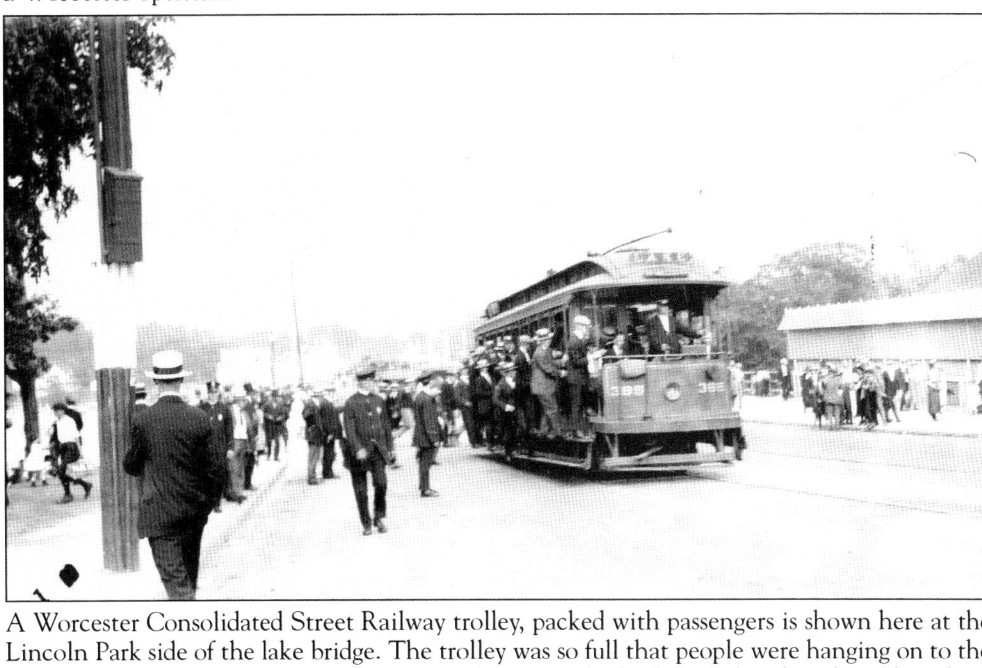

A Worcester Consolidated Street Railway trolley, packed with passengers is shown here at the Lincoln Park side of the lake bridge. The trolley was so full that people were hanging on to the sides. Throngs of people can be seen on the bridge in the background and to the right, where Lincoln Park was located. The police officers in the foreground worked out of a small station located just out of view to the left.

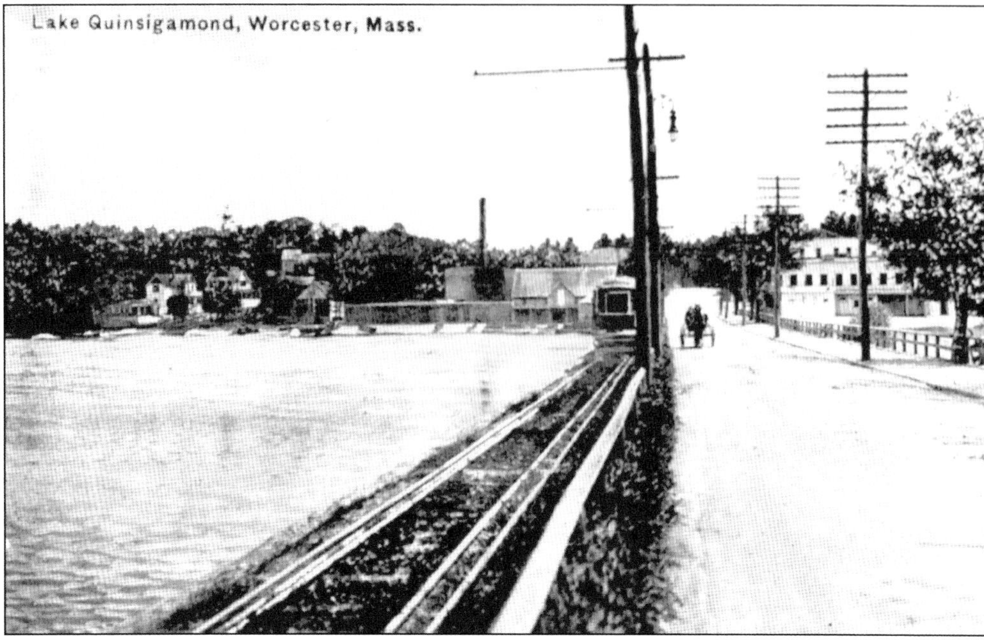

This is a view of the causeway, looking eastward into Shrewsbury. Here we have modern technology, in the form of a trolley car, passing alongside a more ancient horse and buggy. When the causeway was being built, at least one horse and team backed up a little too far while unloading the gravel used to fill in the lake, resulting in the loss of both horse and wagon.

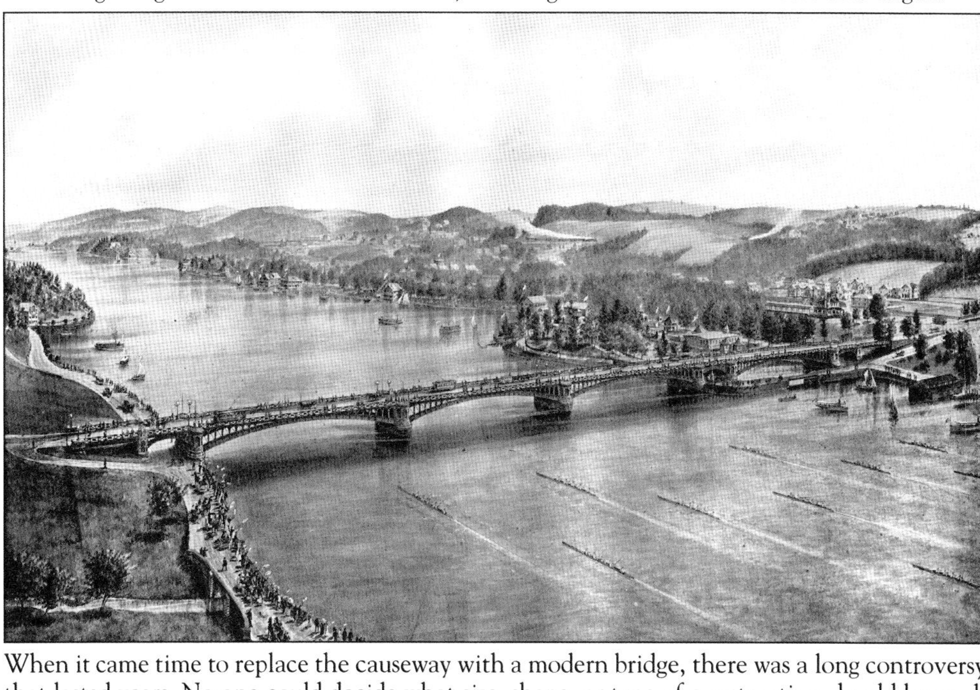

When it came time to replace the causeway with a modern bridge, there was a long controversy that lasted years. No one could decide what size, shape, or type of construction should be used. H. H. Bigelow even had this print produced of a proposed steel bridge. Finally, a concrete bridge was completed in 1919. The print shown here was very lifelike; almost everything was depicted exactly as it stood at the time, with the exception of the bridge itself.

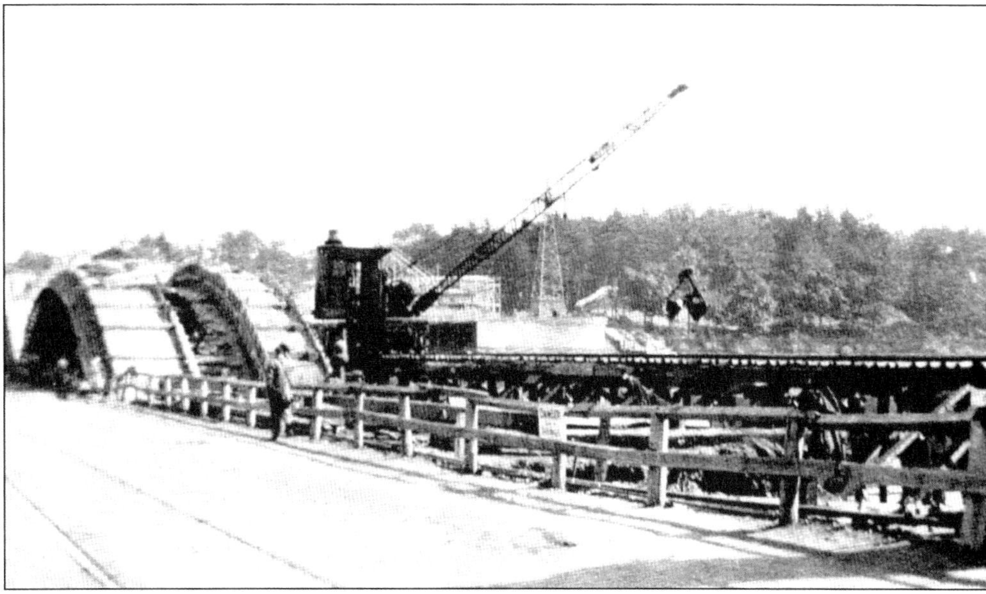

This is a unique view of the Route 9 bridge being built over Lake Quinsigamond. The photographer was standing on the old causeway, looking toward White City Amusement Park, which can just be seen to the right of the crane. The arches of the bridge, under construction, are visible in the left background.

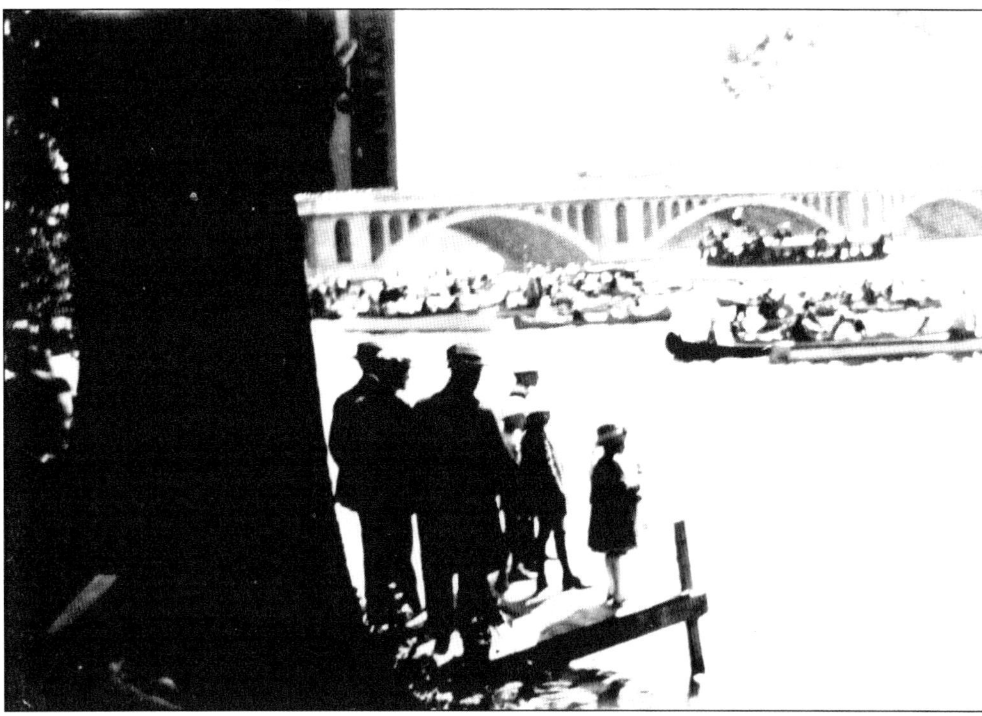

The caption on this photograph reads: "Taken in the year of 1918 after bridge was built. We lived here to see it build" [*sic*]. The little girl on the dock looks to be well dressed for a special occasion. The many boats, including what looks to be a steamboat, indicate that there must have been an event going on, such as a regatta or boat parade.

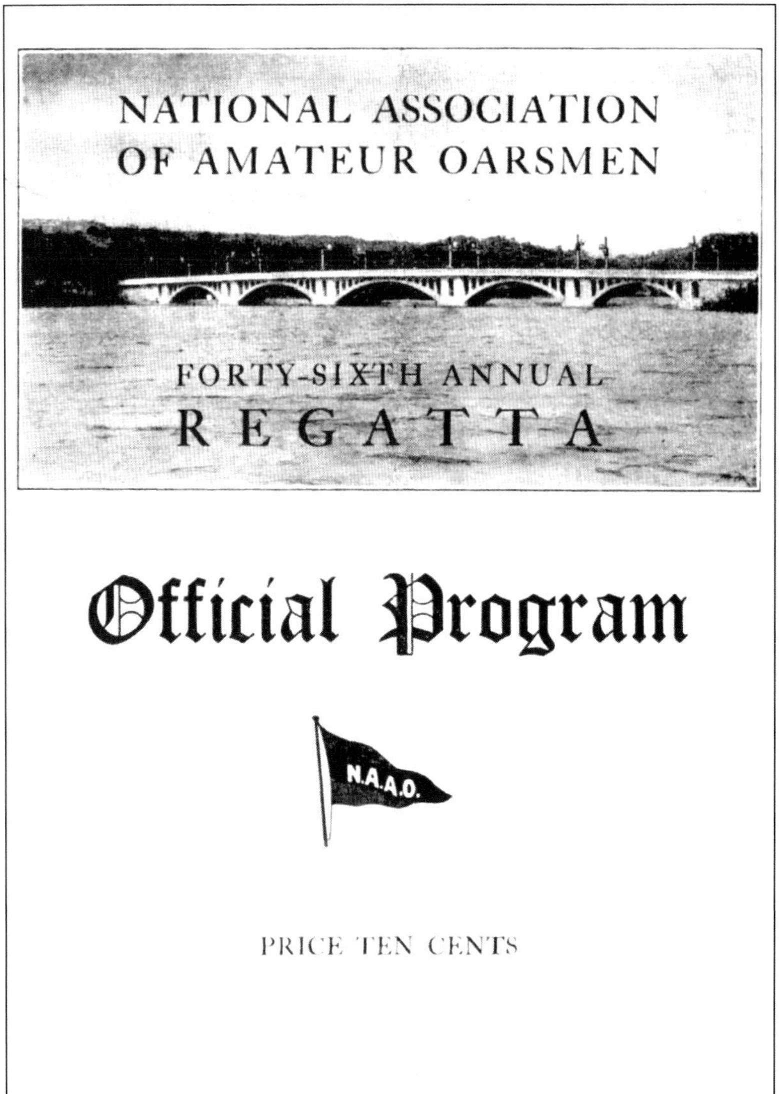
NATIONAL ASSOCIATION
OF AMATEUR OARSMEN

FORTY-SIXTH ANNUAL
REGATTA

Official Program

N.A.A.O.

PRICE TEN CENTS

JULY 23rd *and* 24th, 1920

Lake Quinsigamond, Worcester, Massachusetts

John B. Kelly was a well-known scull rower. In 1919 and 1920 he had won the U.S. National Championship single scull competitions. He was barred from the 1920 Henley Regatta in England, since he was a bricklayer and therefore was not considered an amateur because he earned money working. As everyone knew, British gentlemen of the class that would be entering the Henley Regatta did not labor for money. During the 1920 National Association of Amateur Oarsmen races on Lake Quinsigamond, Kelly won the quarter-mile dash, the championship single, and, along with another rower, the senior double race. Kelly was eventually inducted into the Olympic Hall of Fame, and a statue was erected in his honor. John Kelly, however, never reached the level of celebrity that his daughter achieved. Grace Kelly eventually grew up to be a famous movie star, later known to the entire world as Princess Grace of Monaco.

Crew racing, of course, has been the sport most associated with Lake Quinsigamond since the mid-1800s. The sport did have a few slack periods over the years, but certainly a strong revival in the late 1930s, headed by Ken Burns, brought crew racing back into prominence. Burns, pictured here, organized high school and college competitions, even Olympic tryouts, on the lake. His efforts paid off, and to this day Lake Quinsigamond is the home of numerous crew-racing events each year. Burns was an excellent sculler himself, winning every race he entered between 1922 and 1925. He later became the police chief in Shrewsbury. (Courtesy Nicholas Perrone, Perrone's Barber Shop.)

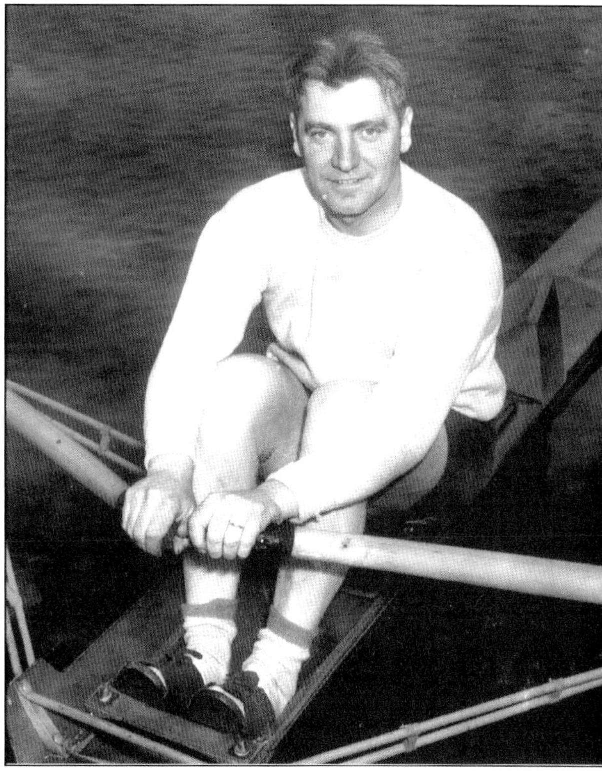

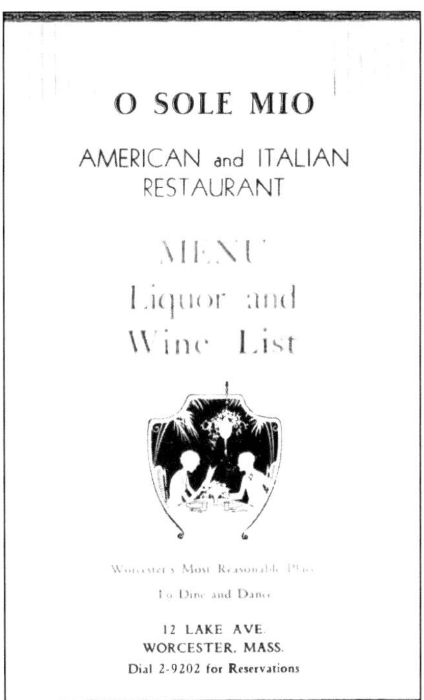

Owned by the DiLiddo family, the O Sole Mio was one of the many restaurants and hot dog stands that lined Lake Avenue opposite Lincoln Park. The O Sole Mio was divided into two parts—one that catered to people who wanted hot dogs, and the other side for people who wanted sit-down meals. This menu lists several Italian offerings, including seven different spaghetti dishes ranging in price from 25 cents to 60 cents. The DiLiddo family sold the business in 1955, and the building burned down the following year.

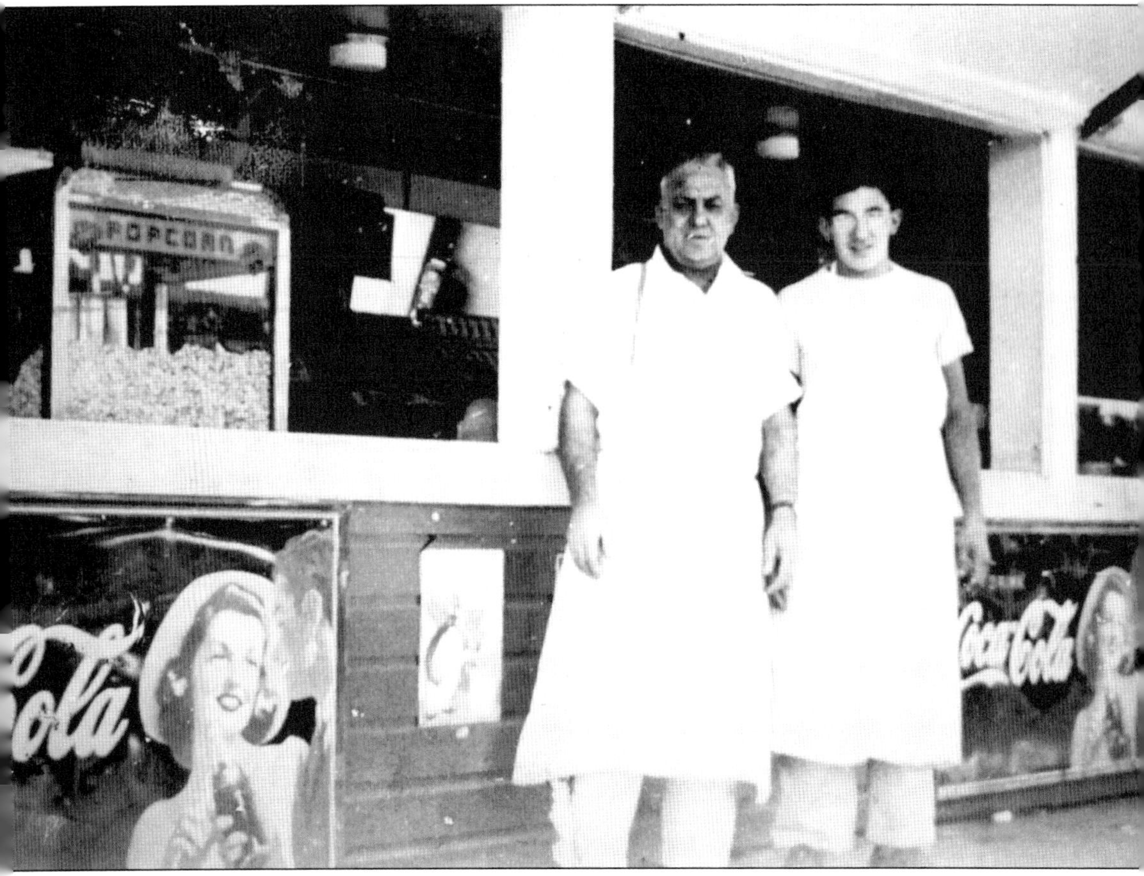

Along with its neighbor, Corey's Hot Dogs, the O Sole Mio did a booming hot dog business in the summer months. It was not unusual for crowds of hungry people to line up for hot dogs, even late at night after both Lincoln Park and White City closed. One family member relates that, at times, people would be turned away at 2 a.m. or 3 a.m. Corey's remained very popular into the 1970s, and parking spaces were hard to find on a summer's night. Pictured here in front of one of the stands are two of the restaurant workers who served up hot dogs to hungry patrons.

Two

WHITE CITY AMUSEMENT PARK

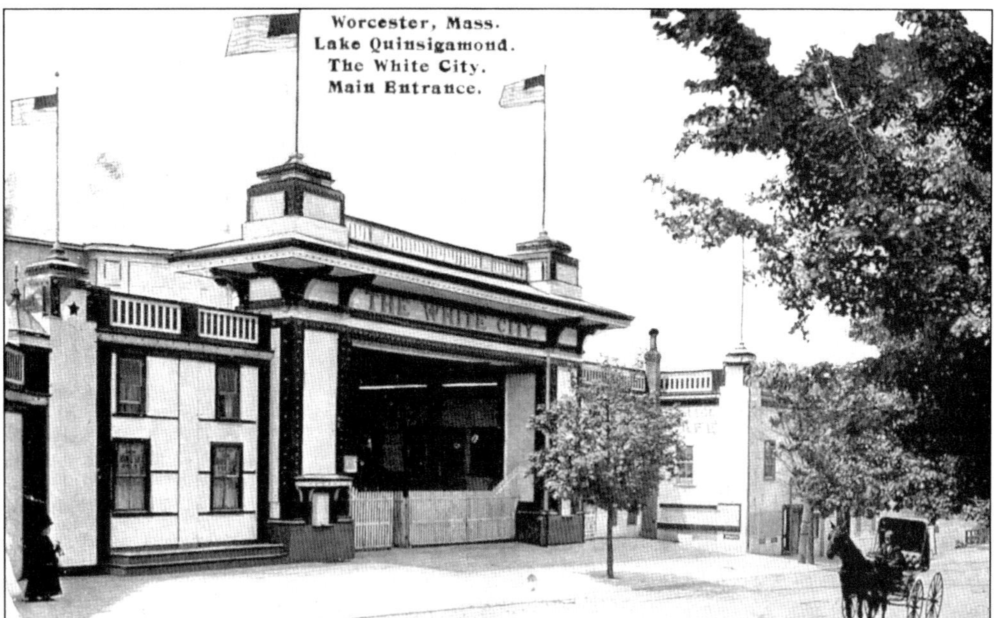

The main entrance to White City Park, facing the Boston and Worcester Turnpike, is shown here. This is where people taking the trolleys or crossing over the causeway from Worcester would enter the park before automobiles became popular. This building shows the white paint scheme that was used throughout the park in the early days.

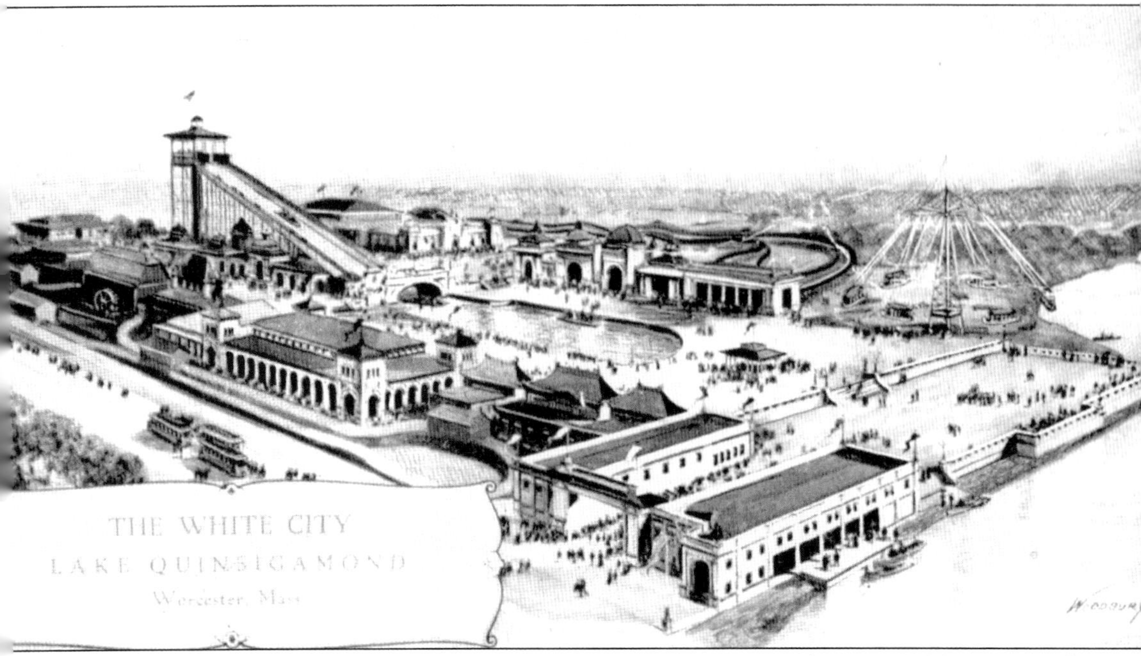

Here is an artist's rendition of the new White City Amusement Park c. 1905. Of interest is the advertising on the reverse of the card, which states the park will open on May 22, 1905. Due to disputes with workmen, the opening of the park was delayed until the following month, making these cards somewhat obsolete.

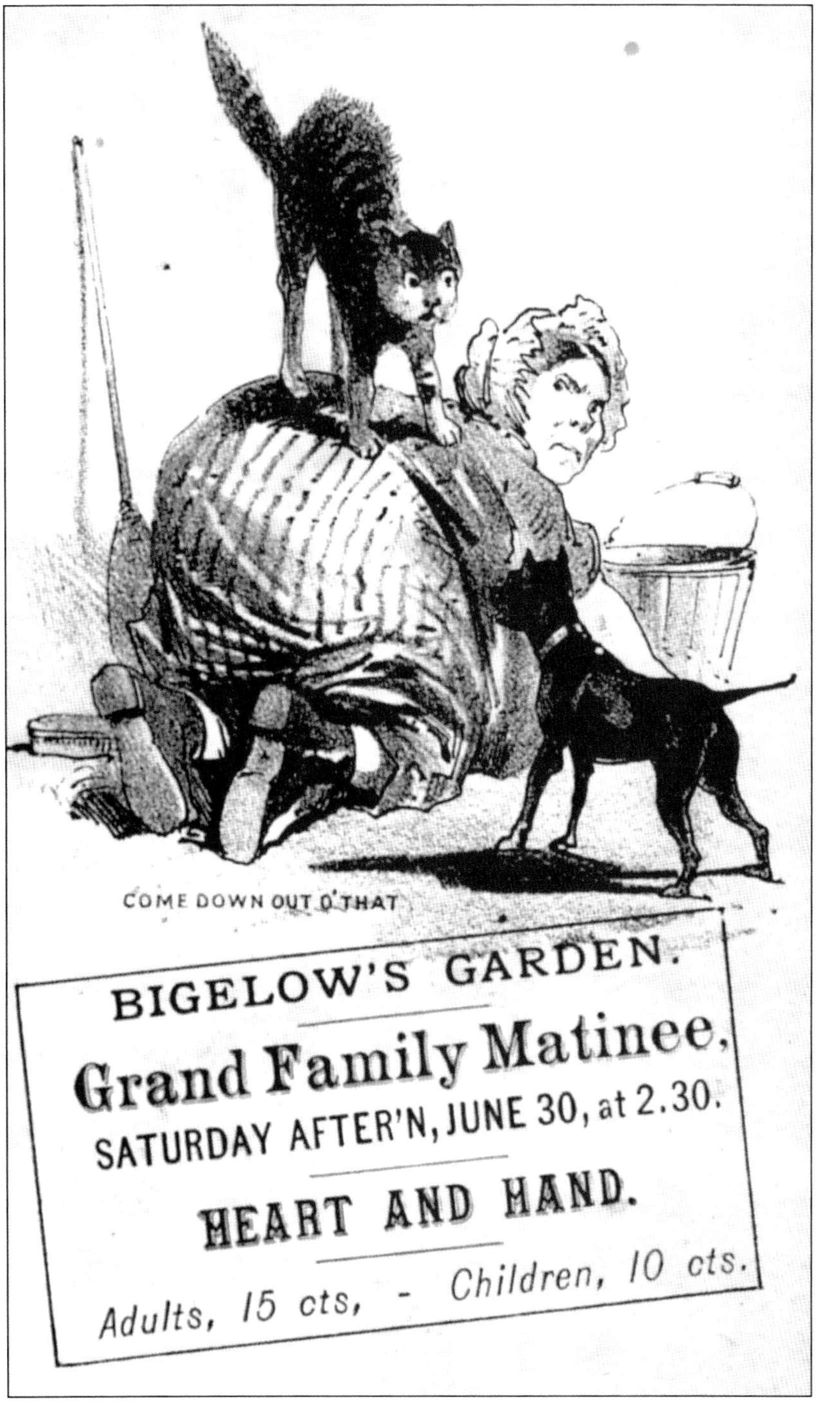

In 1881, Horace H. Bigelow, who later built White City Amusement Park, bought a huge roller-skating rink in downtown Worcester. He then added Bigelow's Garden, featuring fountains and gardens, to the facility. Bigelow ran into trouble with the city fathers when he began holding concerts on Sundays. The city sued to stop the concerts, but the case was eventually dropped. An advertising card for a grand family matinee at the garden is shown here.

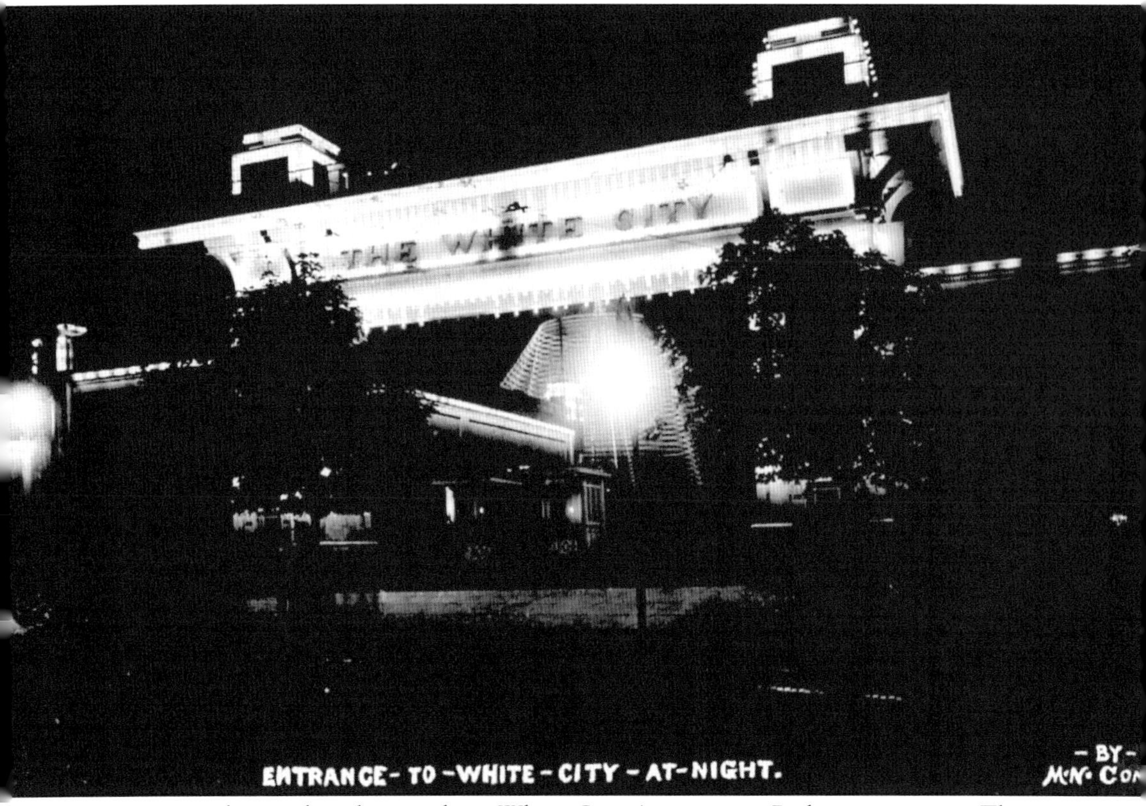

Many people wonder where or how White City Amusement Park got its name. The name originated with the 1893 Columbian Exposition in Chicago, Illinois. At the exposition there was a grand exhibit that featured buildings painted bright white, which were illuminated at night by a multitude of electric lights—the White City. Electric light was a new invention at that time, and the light reflecting off the white buildings was spectacular to people who had never seen a light bulb, much less a large display of them. The name White City was later adopted by amusement parks throughout the country that used the same theme of brightly lit white buildings. Fascination with the electric light resulted in many nighttime postcard views of White City parks.

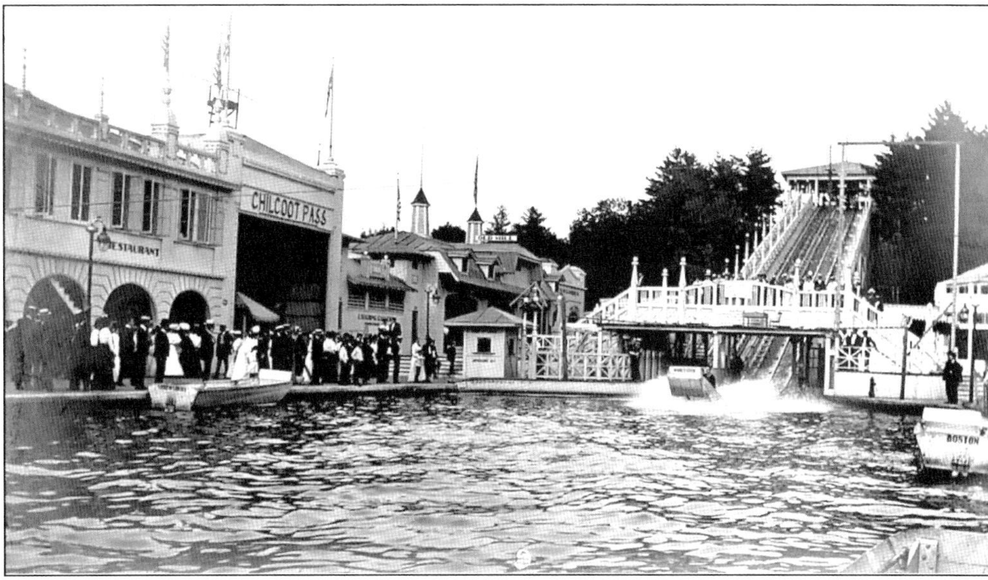

This photograph from a postcard was taken only one month after the White City Park opened, on July 22, 1905. The boats used on the Shoot the Chutes ride were each named after a city or town. To the left is the Chilcoot Pass building, advertised with the slogan, "It only takes a nickel to get in, but a long time to get out!"

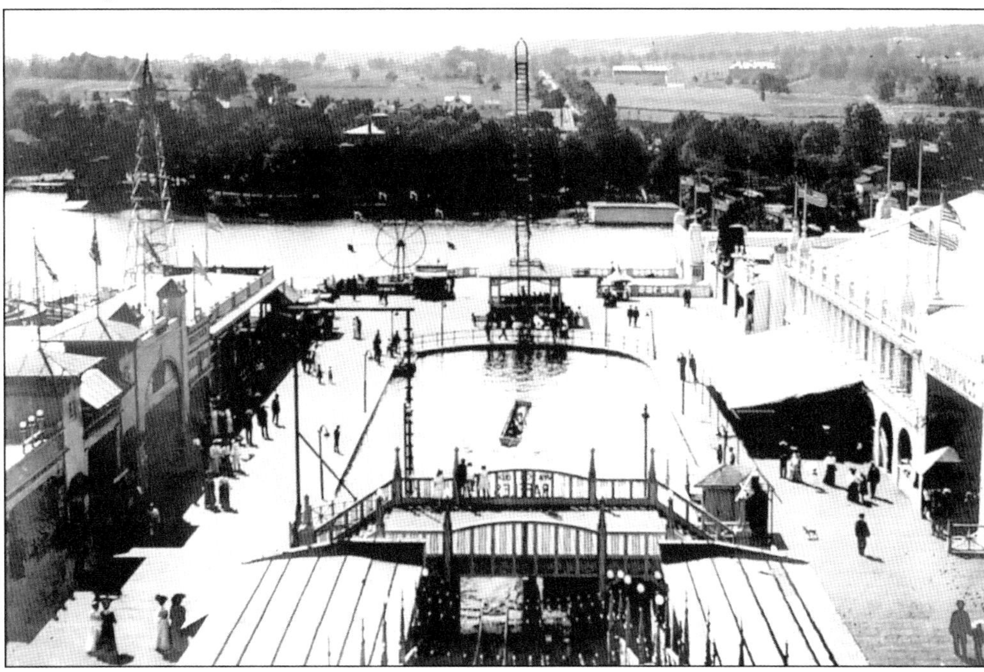

This photograph was taken from the top of the Shoot the Chutes ride. The picture shows the layout of the boardwalk, or Pike area of the park, as it existed from 1905 to the late 1920s. The Whirl of Captive Airships ride is on the left, close to the lake, and the park's bandstand is at the end of the pool, with various attractions on each side. The empty landscape in the far distance to the south is now the heavily populated Lake View area of Worcester; to the north is where the University of Massachusetts Hospital complex now stands.

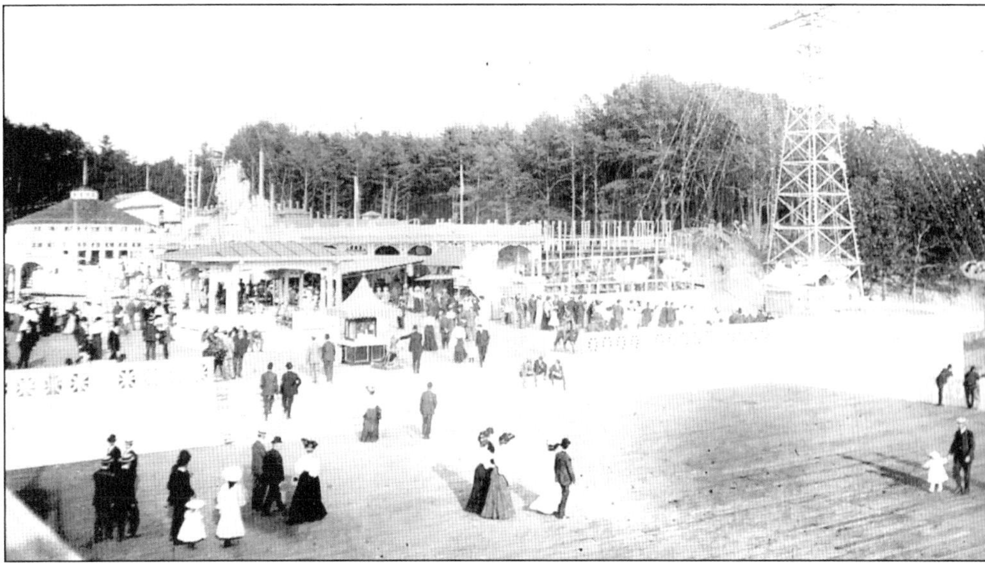

The Worcester Photo Company published this overall view of White City. It gives an excellent idea of the layout of the park in its early configuration. The carousel building, King Dodo, the bandstand, part of the boardwalk, Whirl of Captive Airships, and the scenic railway ride can be recognized. The area in the foreground bordered on the lake shore.

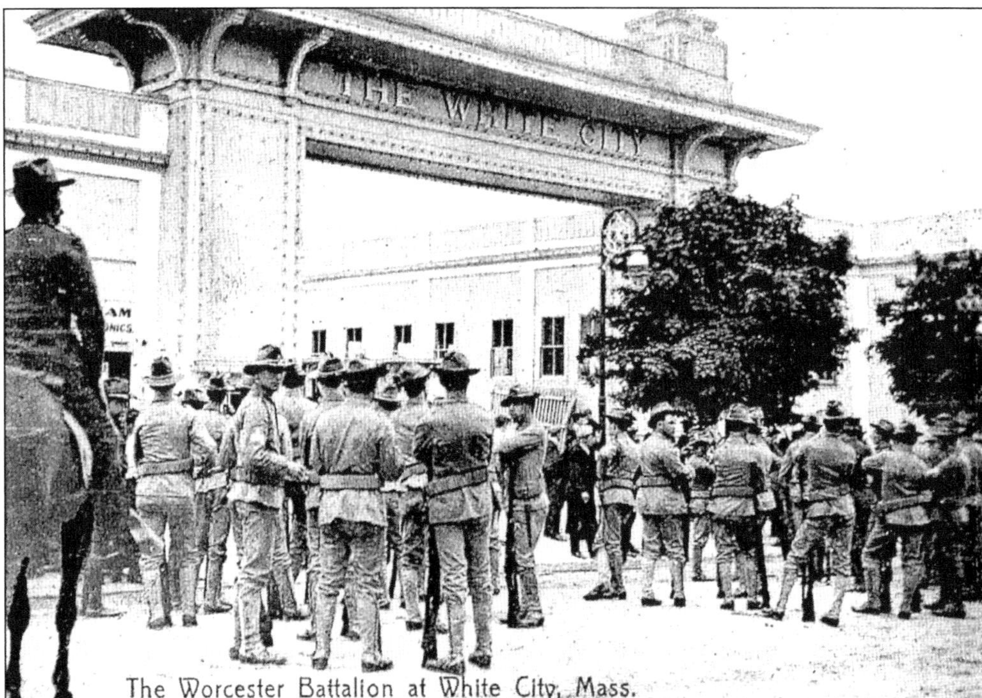

This unusual postcard shows a group of soldiers standing at the main entrance to White City c. 1905. These soldiers most likely were members of some of the National Guard units based in the area. It was very common for these units to use the rifle range located off West Main Street in Shrewsbury. One woman who grew up near there remembers the soldiers going to White City on Saturday nights of weekend encampments.

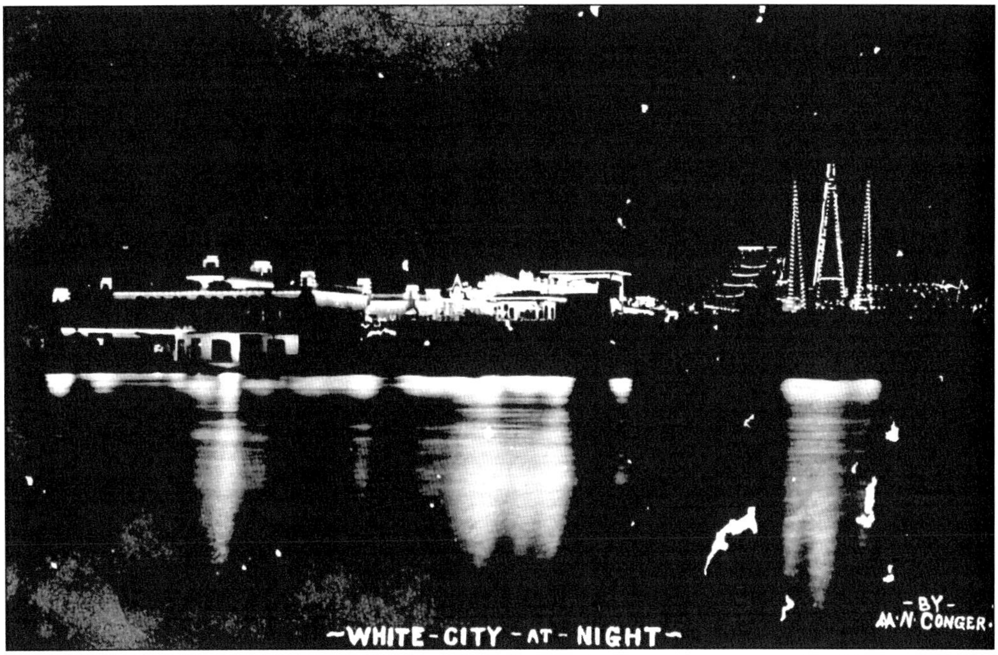

This is another nighttime shot, which shows the park from the water side. This particular photograph was taken by M. N. Conger, who was a prolific photographer of scenes at Lake Quinsigamond. Some of his postcard views, allegedly taken at night, may have been shot during the day using filters to make it look like nighttime.

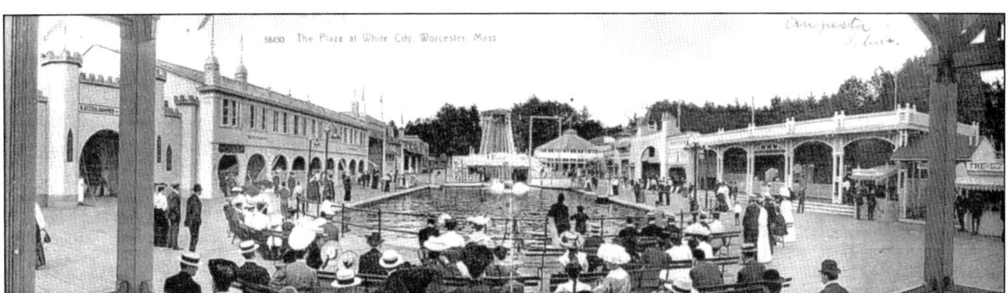

This rare panoramic postcard shows the entire boardwalk area at White City c. 1909. The image shows the boardwalk area as it would be viewed from the bandstand, looking toward the Shoot the Chutes. It is interesting to note that very few children are among the people in this scene; the park appealed more to youngsters as time went by.

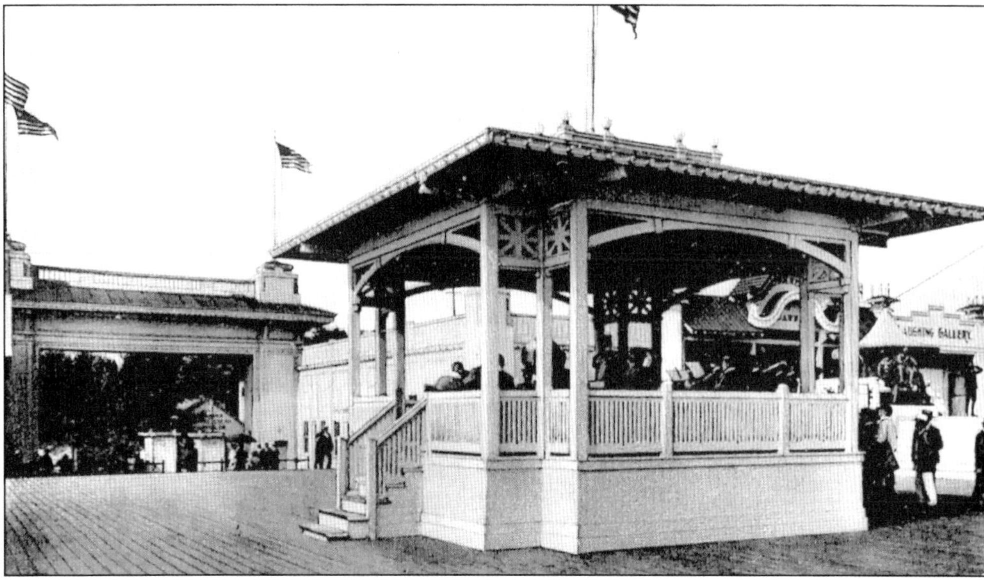

The White City bandstand was placed in a convenient spot, just west of Fairy Lake—the man-made pool used for the Shoot the Chutes ride. Music was provided at various times, both during the day and at night, for people strolling on the boardwalk or sitting and watching the variety of activities. The bandstand was removed during later renovations of the park.

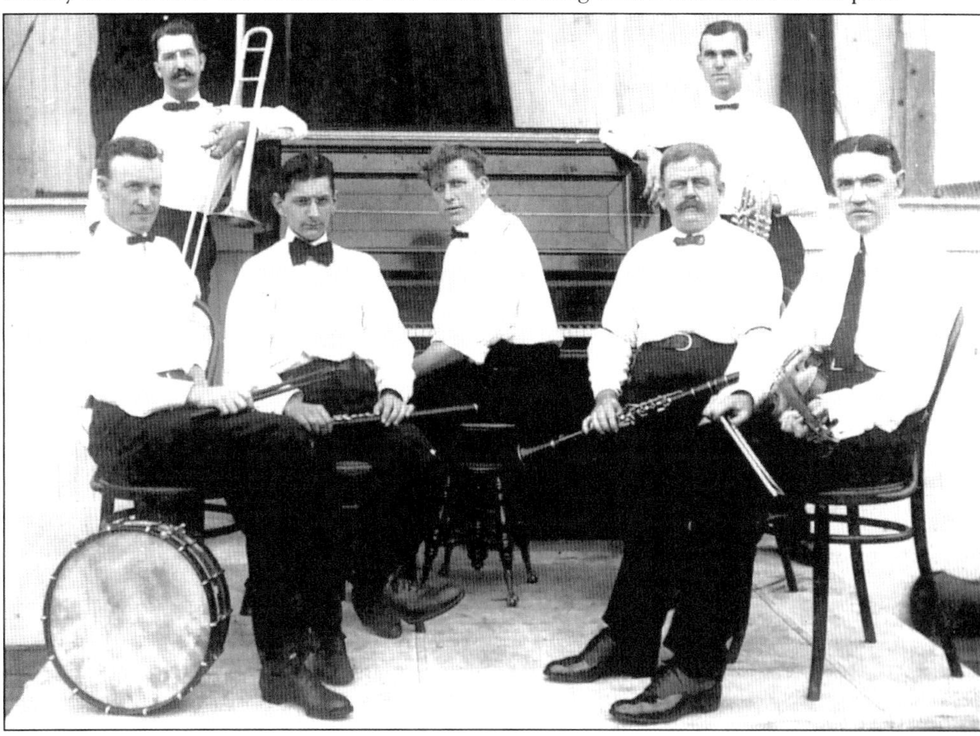

The Wallace and Hagney Orchestra, shown here, was one of several musical groups that performed during the early days of White City. This particular group provided the music in the dance hall. The orchestra was billed as "rendering the most popular and pleasing music every afternoon and evening." (Courtesy Barton Kamp.)

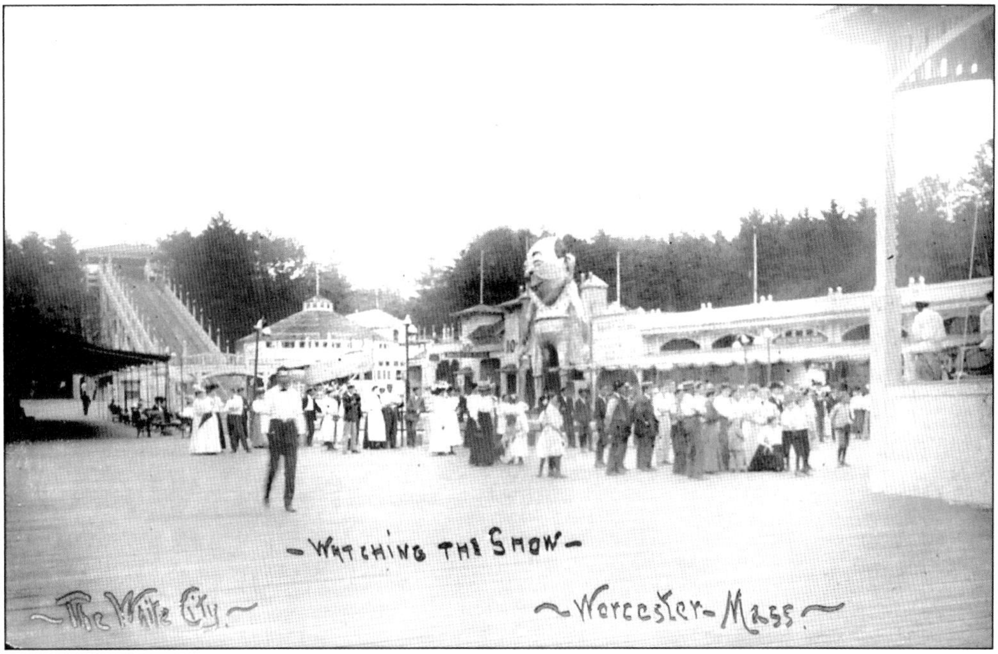

This crowd of onlookers is watching a show in progress on the White City bandstand, which stood just at the south end of the Shoot the Chutes man-made pool. Band concerts were just one of the many types of free entertainment offered in the early days of the park, during White City's ongoing battle for customers with Lincoln Park across the lake. (Courtesy Barton Kamp.)

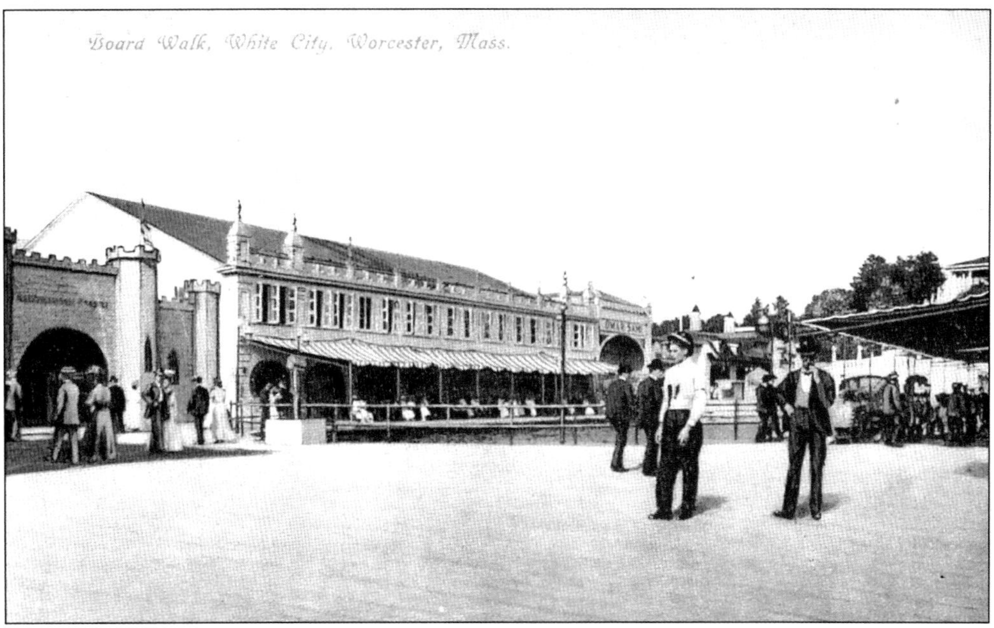

The boardwalk at White City encircled the Fairy Lake. This promenade at the center of the park allowed people to stop at any of the many attractions arrayed around it. Some visitors would sit and watch the Shoot the Chutes boats hurtling down the ramp into the water, while others enjoyed free shows or fireworks displays. The boardwalk remained for the most part intact even after the renovations of the 1920s, but it was removed during subsequent modernizations.

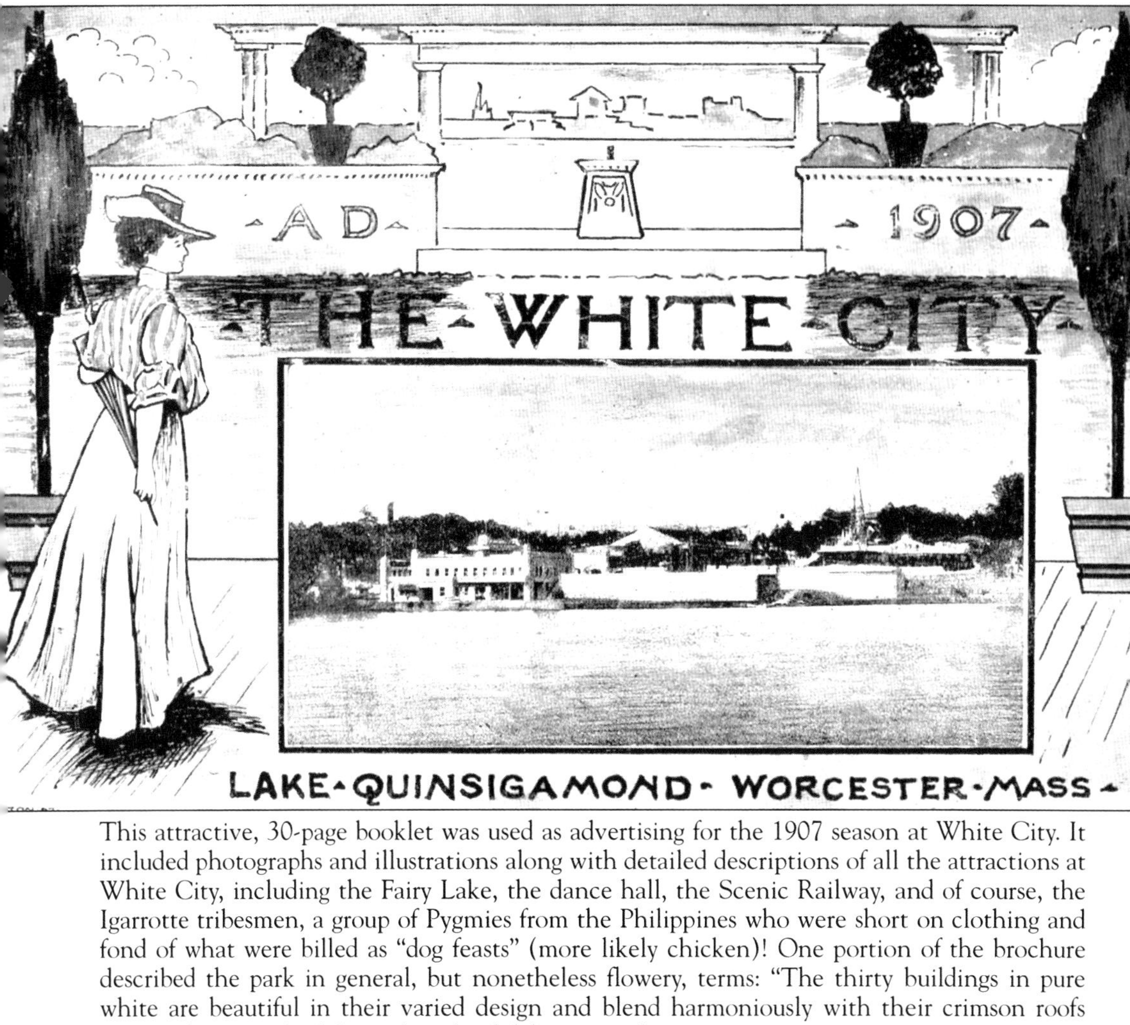

This attractive, 30-page booklet was used as advertising for the 1907 season at White City. It included photographs and illustrations along with detailed descriptions of all the attractions at White City, including the Fairy Lake, the dance hall, the Scenic Railway, and of course, the Igarrotte tribesmen, a group of Pygmies from the Philippines who were short on clothing and fond of what were billed as "dog feasts" (more likely chicken)! One portion of the brochure described the park in general, but nonetheless flowery, terms: "The thirty buildings in pure white are beautiful in their varied design and blend harmoniously with their crimson roofs against the green backdrop of a splendid fine grove."

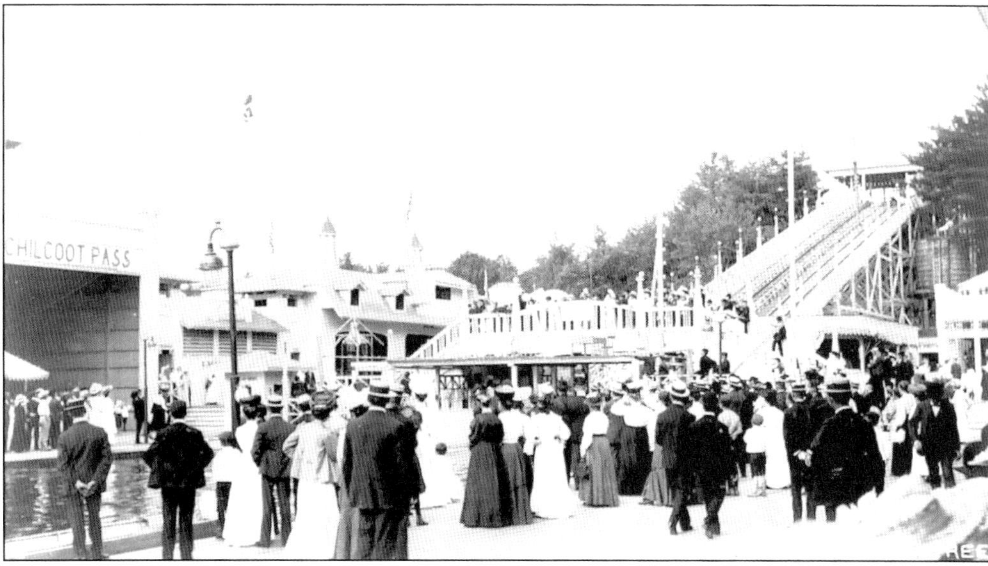

This postcard shows crowds of people walking on the boardwalk at White City. Across the Fairy Lake is the entrance to the Chilcoot Pass attraction. A description in a brochure gives few clues about what this ride might have been like: "Don't fail to visit Chilcoot Pass and be a boy again to your heart's content. More fun than you ever had before, whether you ride or watch others ride." (Courtesy Barton Kamp.)

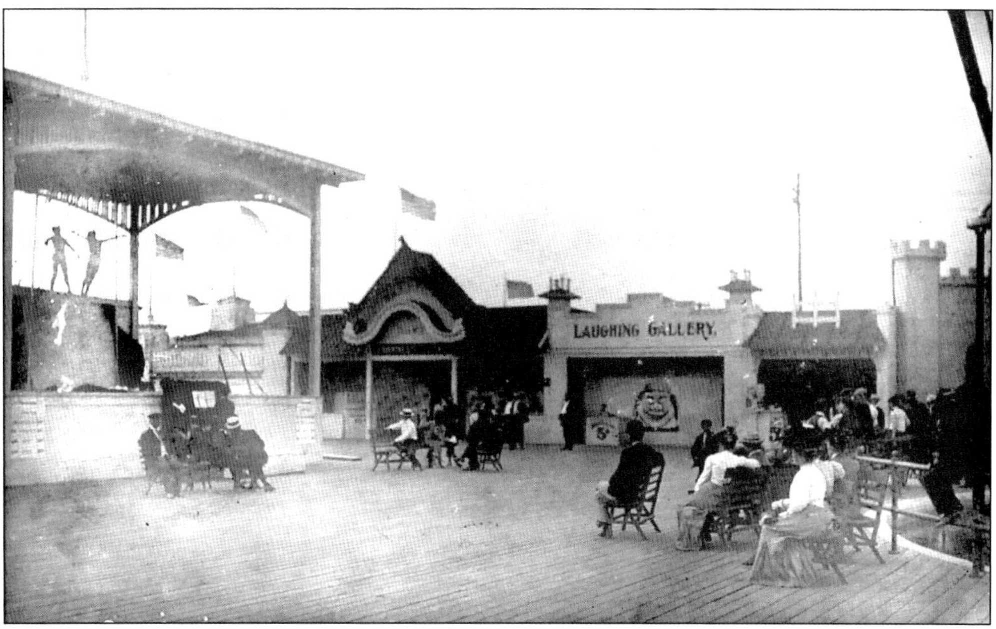

This postcard view shows the Laughing Gallery, another of the park's original attractions. It was described as follows: "Have a good laugh in the Laughing Gallery. See how you might have looked if you had grown differently." An accompanying illustration shows a man looking into a mirror that makes his face look long and drawn, his body compressed, with long spindly legs protruding. (Courtesy Barton Kamp.)

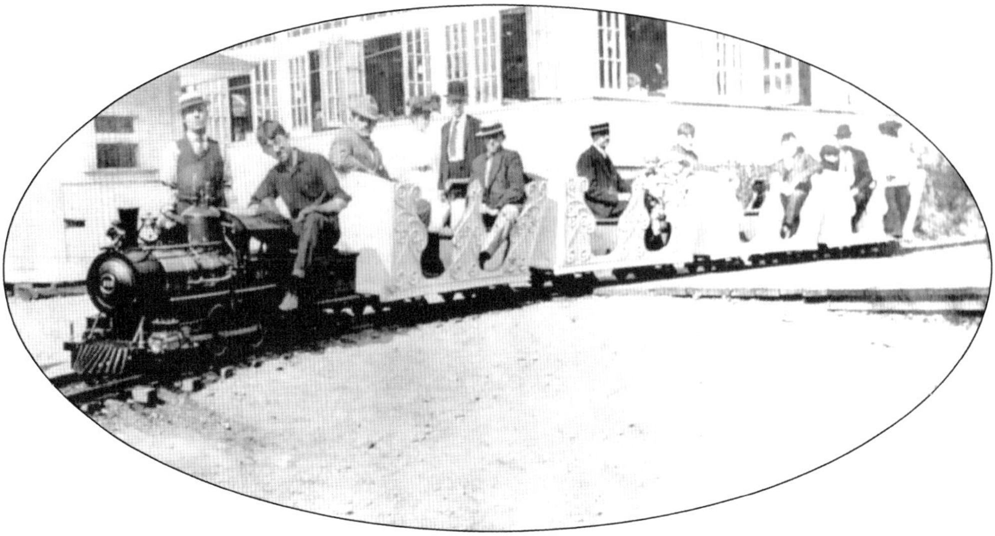

This is a photo-postcard view of the miniature train that ran at White City. It carried full-size passengers, although the train itself was described as being "drawn by a midget locomotive 5 feet long and 28 inches high, burning miniature coal" and having a "Midget Engineer and Conductor." The little engine recently surfaced and was sold for a sizeable amount through an online auction. (Courtesy Barton Kamp.)

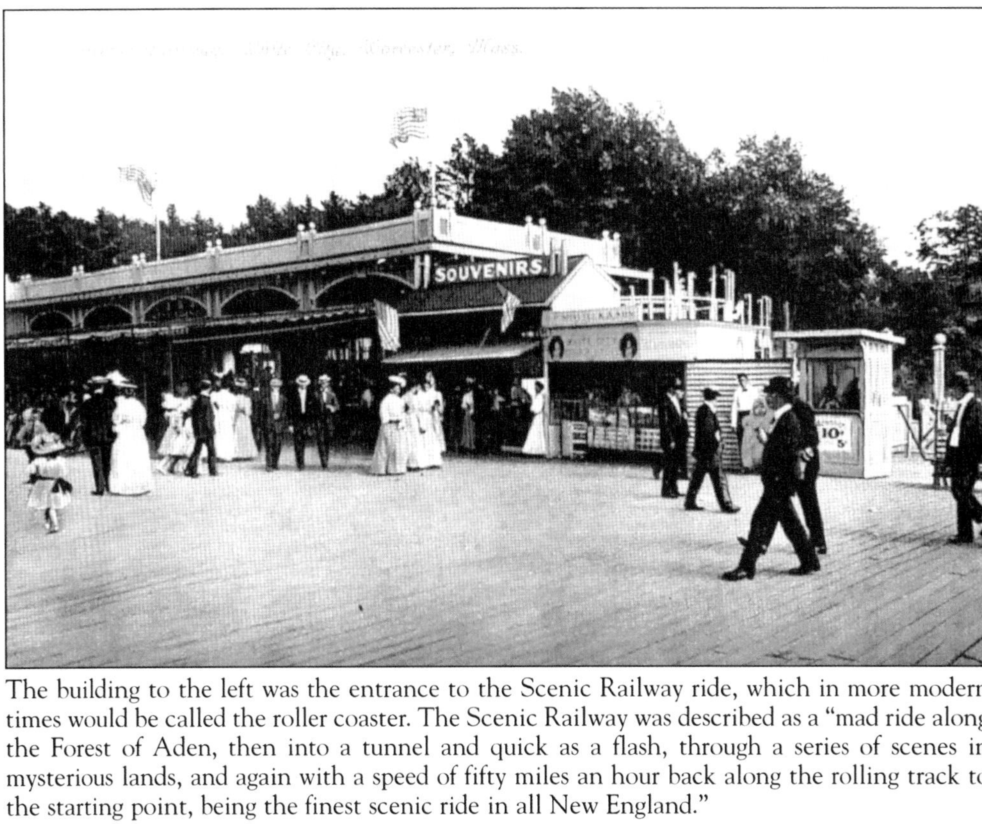

The building to the left was the entrance to the Scenic Railway ride, which in more modern times would be called the roller coaster. The Scenic Railway was described as a "mad ride along the Forest of Aden, then into a tunnel and quick as a flash, through a series of scenes in mysterious lands, and again with a speed of fifty miles an hour back along the rolling track to the starting point, being the finest scenic ride in all New England."

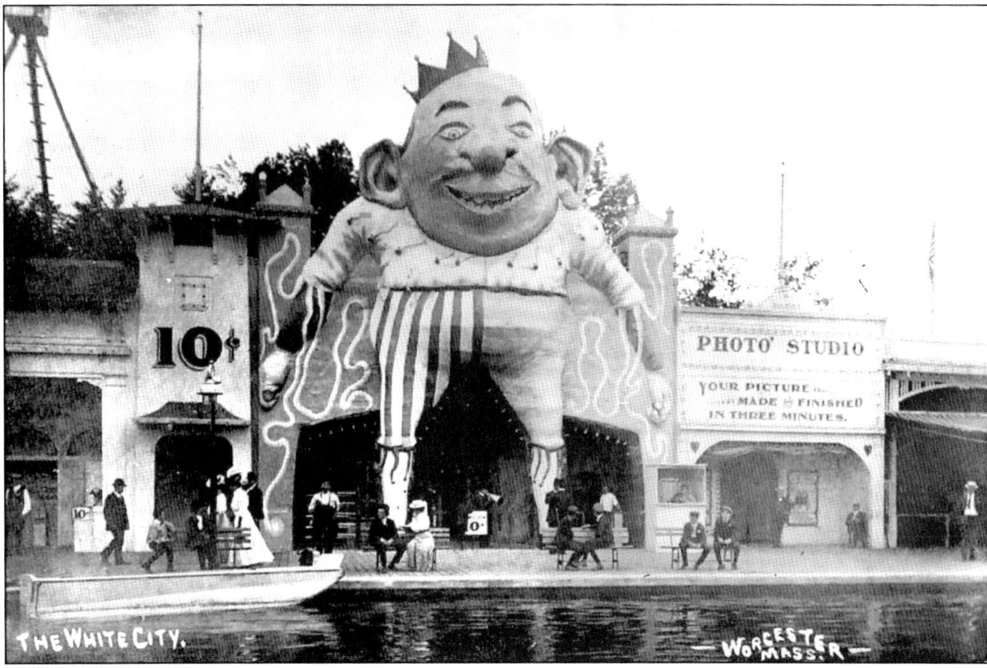

King Dodo's Palace is the subject of this photograph by the Worcester Photo Company. King Dodo himself was featured during the early years of White City. The entrance to a fun house–type building was between King Dodo's legs. An early version of a photograph studio ("Your picture made and finished in three minutes") is located just to the right of King Dodo. This card bears the message "Aug. 17 – 1906. We went to White City. All had a fine time."

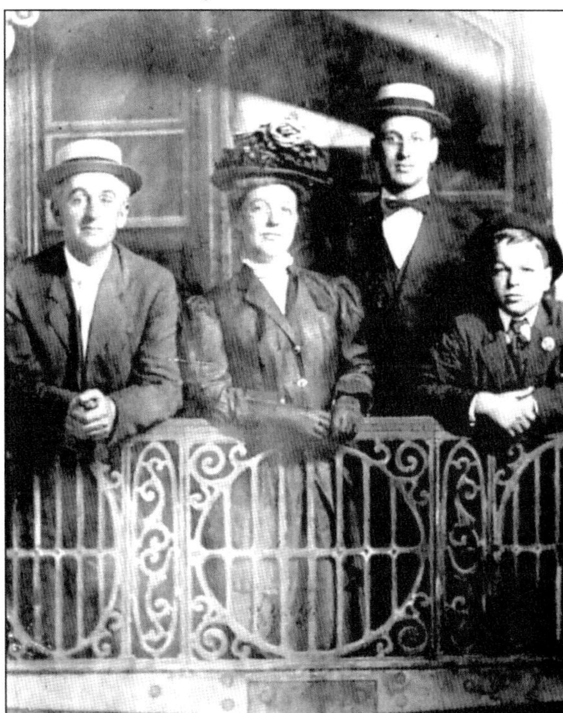

This group of visitors to White City had their picture taken at the King Dodo's Palace photography studio in 1905. The studio's sign advertised that photographs could be taken and finished in three minutes—quite an achievement for its day! The postcard even has a White City post office logo on the reverse side. (Courtesy Erik Larson.)

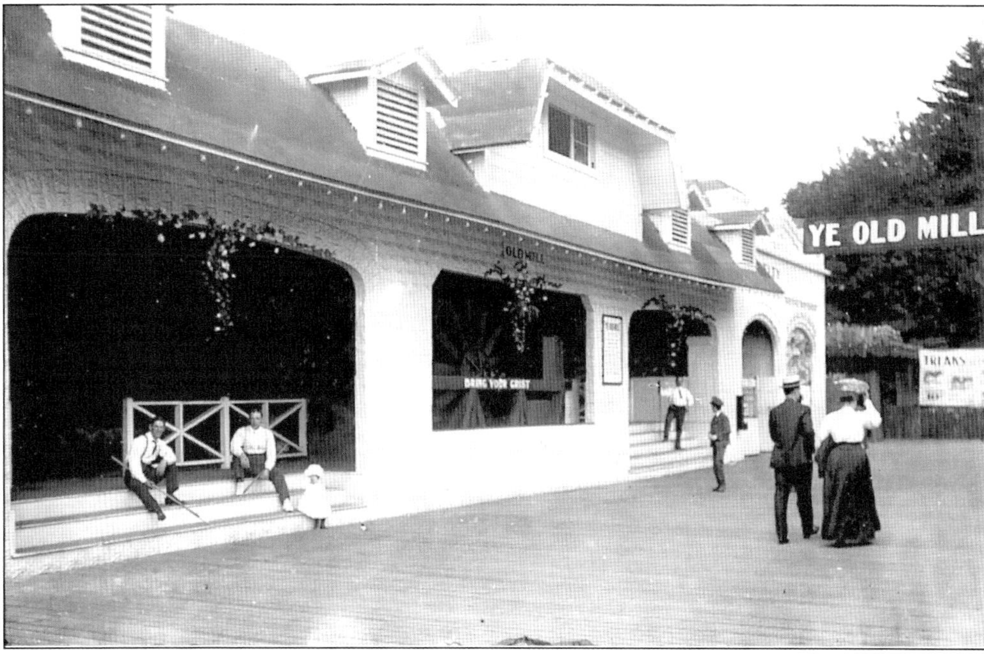

This view shows the building that housed Ye Old Mill. This was one of the park's original attractions in 1905. It was described in an advertising brochure published in anticipation of the park's opening: "The Old Mill, with its stream of water flowing in its sinuous course amid scenes of tropic luxuriance and frigid grandeur, is a most popular ride around the grounds." Although there is no way to tell for sure, the ride may have consisted of small boats pulled through a course around the park. (Courtesy Barton Kamp.)

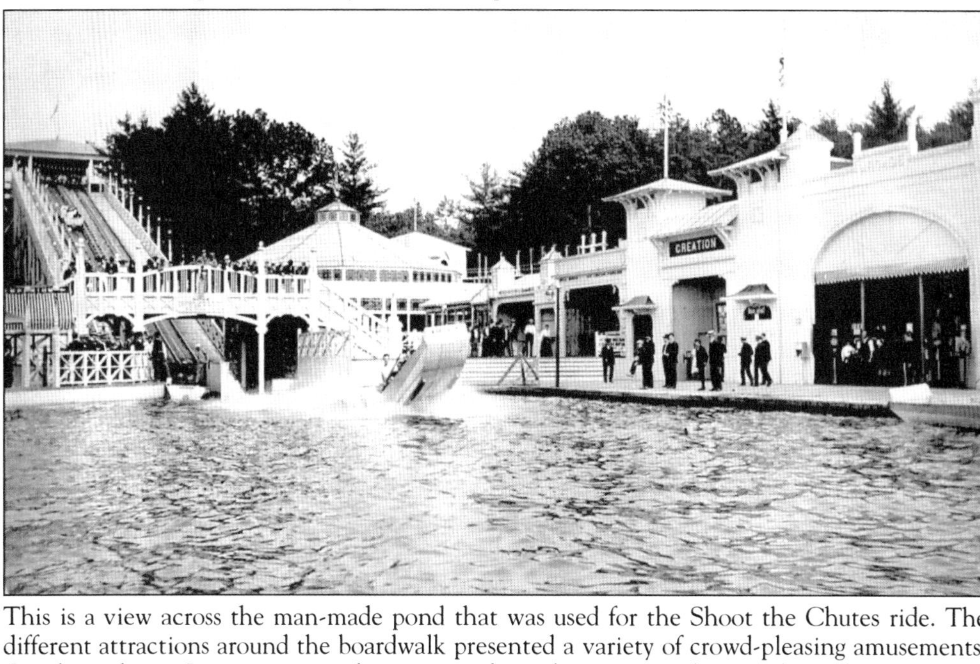

This is a view across the man-made pond that was used for the Shoot the Chutes ride. The different attractions around the boardwalk presented a variety of crowd-pleasing amusements. On the right is Creation, an early version of an electric map showing how the world was created. The circular-shaped building at the center housed White City's carousel.

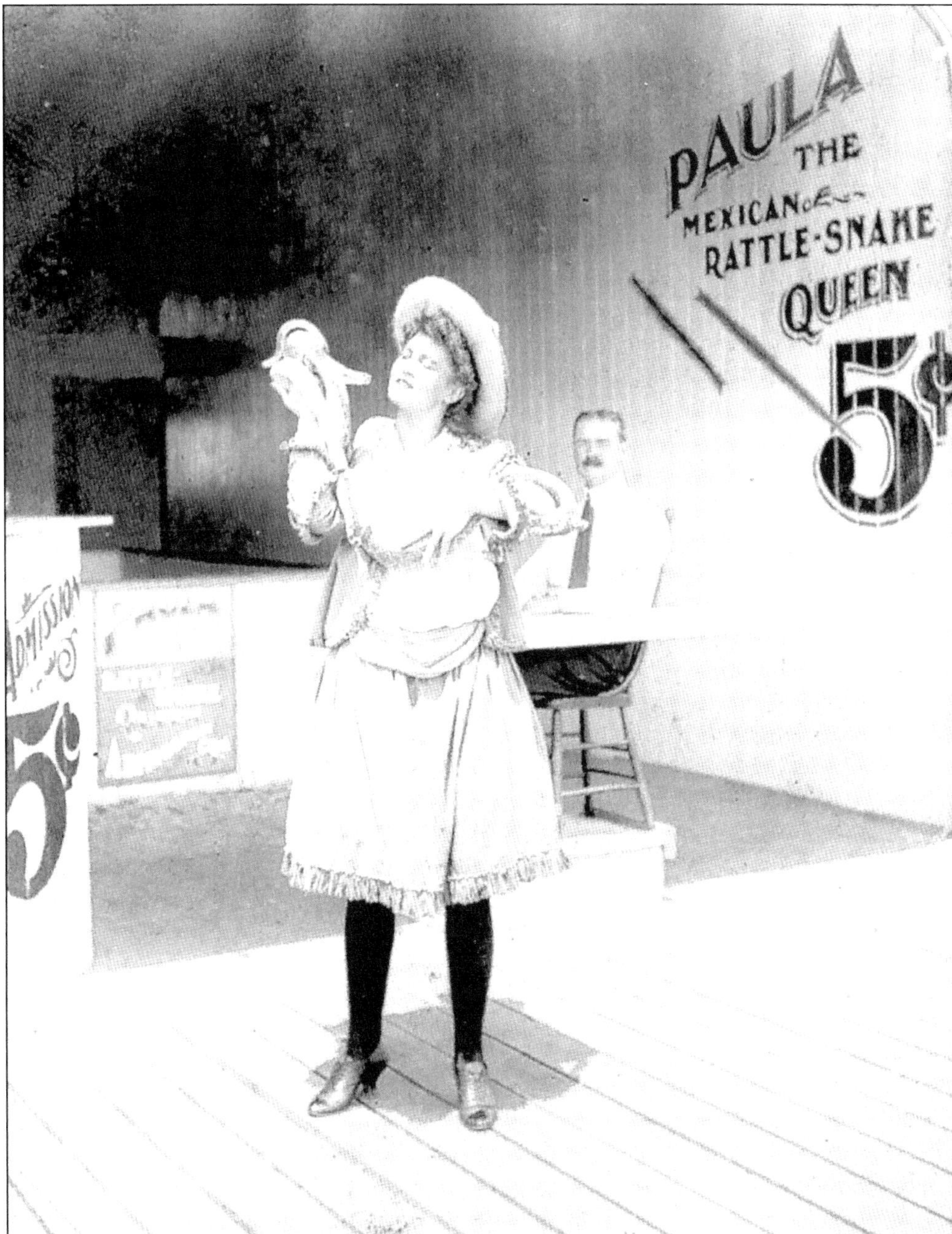

White City had many sideshow attractions, especially in the earlier years. Dancing bears, diving horses, high divers and trapeze artists, and various oddities (some real, some surely man-made) all served to attract the interest of paying customers. Many of these attractions remain mysteries, like the one advertised as "The Unknown," for instance. Paula the Mexican Rattlesnake Queen, a classic sideshow act if there ever was one, is shown posing with her snake in this Worcester Photo Company postcard view from 1906. Many of the park's sideshows were invented during the era of the famous showman P. T. Barnum, who said, "There's a sucker born every minute." (Courtesy Erik Larson.)

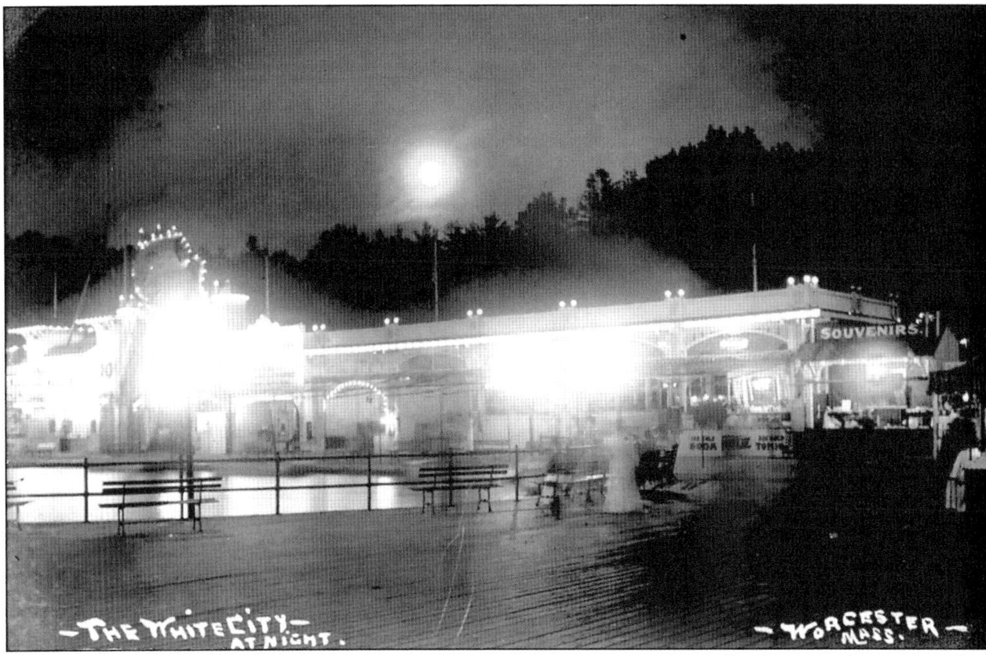

At night, White City presented a spectacular appearance, especially for people in the days before electric lights became common household appliances. This view of the boardwalk area shows the many strings of lights used to illuminate the park, including some draped over King Dodo. (Courtesy Erik Larson.)

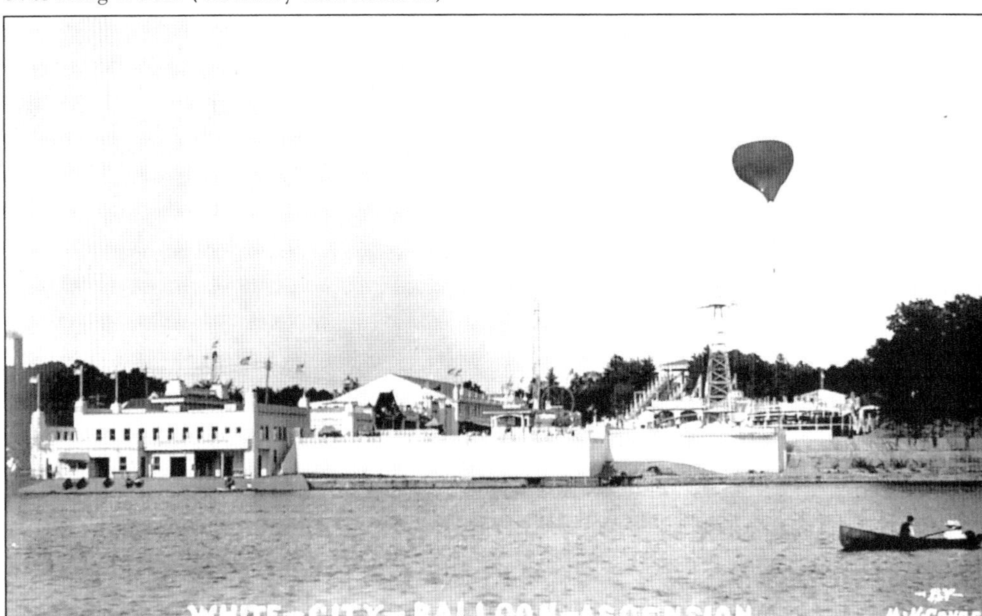

Balloon ascensions were a popular attraction at the lake, although they were not frequent. This view shows a balloon floating along over White City. One balloon ascension in the 1890s was documented by the local paper: The balloon's operator, probably in an attempt to glamorize the whole affair, claimed he went so high that he actually saw a man being arrested on Boston Common for pickpocketing! (Courtesy Barton Kamp.)

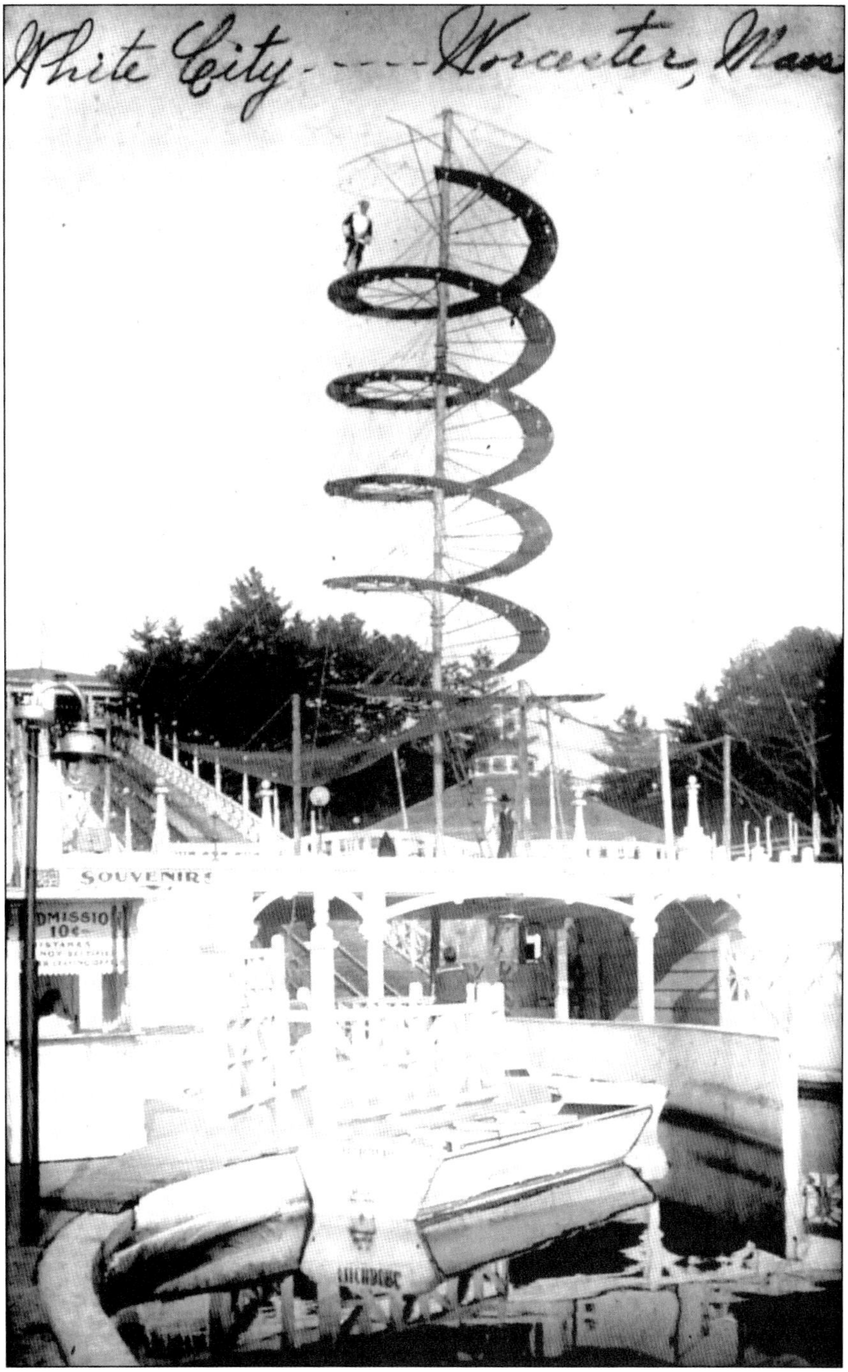

One of the many special attractions at White City is shown here. This contraption was most likely used by a bicycle rider, who would thrill the crowds while descending on the circular ramp. Competition for customers was fierce between Lincoln Park and White City, and special shows like this were used as a means to entice people to visit the respective parks. On summer weekends, the causeway, and later the Route 9 bridge, were packed with crowds of people going back and forth between the parks. (Courtesy Barton Kamp.)

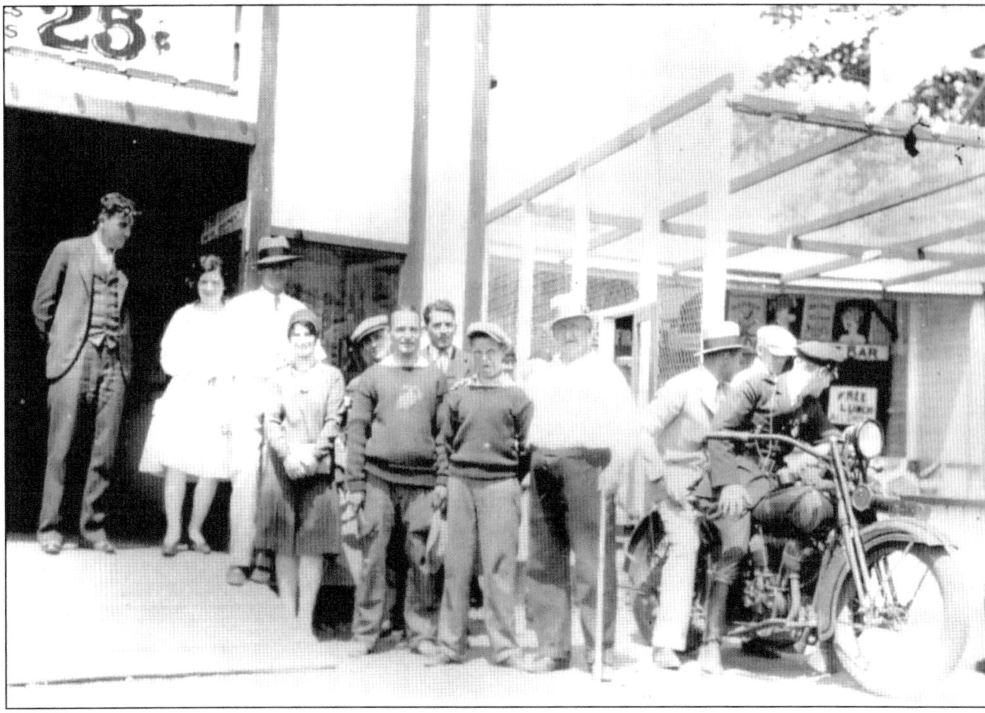

Here we have a group of people who worked at White City, passing some time with a motorcycle policeman. Although this patrolman was a regular member of the Shrewsbury Police Department, other officers were hired just to work at White City; indeed, an example of a White City police badge still exists. Many neighborhood people worked at rides or concessions during the summer, and some would stay on over the winter, performing maintenance on the rides or buildings.

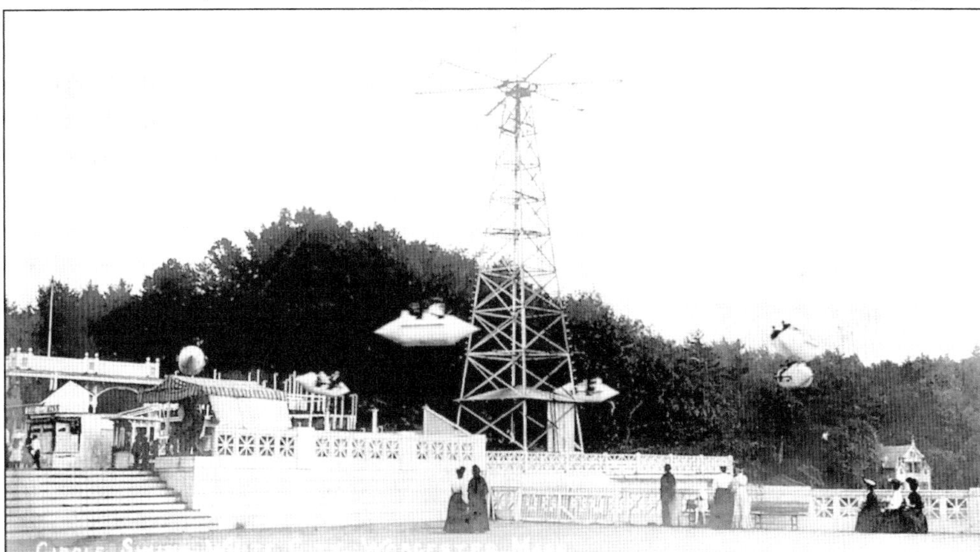

A ride that endured from the first days of White City until it closed was first known as the Whirl of Captive Airships. When rocket ships became a reality, the ride was modernized with gleaming chrome rockets that had engines in the rear, unlike like these earlier models that were pointy at both ends.

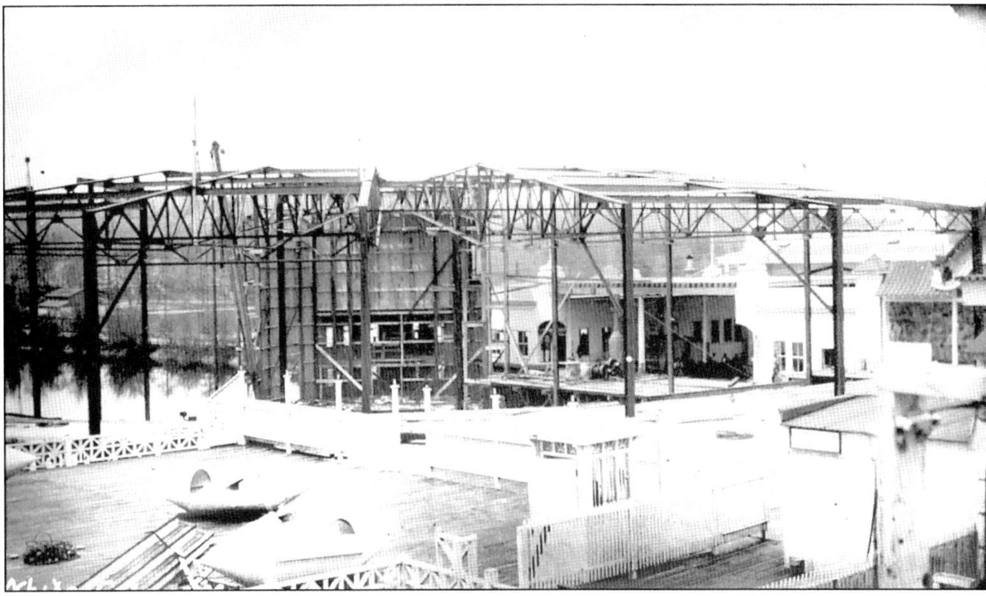

This is an early blue and white–tone photograph showing the dance hall area of the park being built. This image can be dated to sometime between the earliest years of the park and 1918, when the present bridge over Lake Quinsigamond was erected, as the dirt causeway can be seen in the left background. Also of interest are the rocket ships, visible in the foreground, that were part of the Whirl of Captive Airships ride that swung out over the lake.

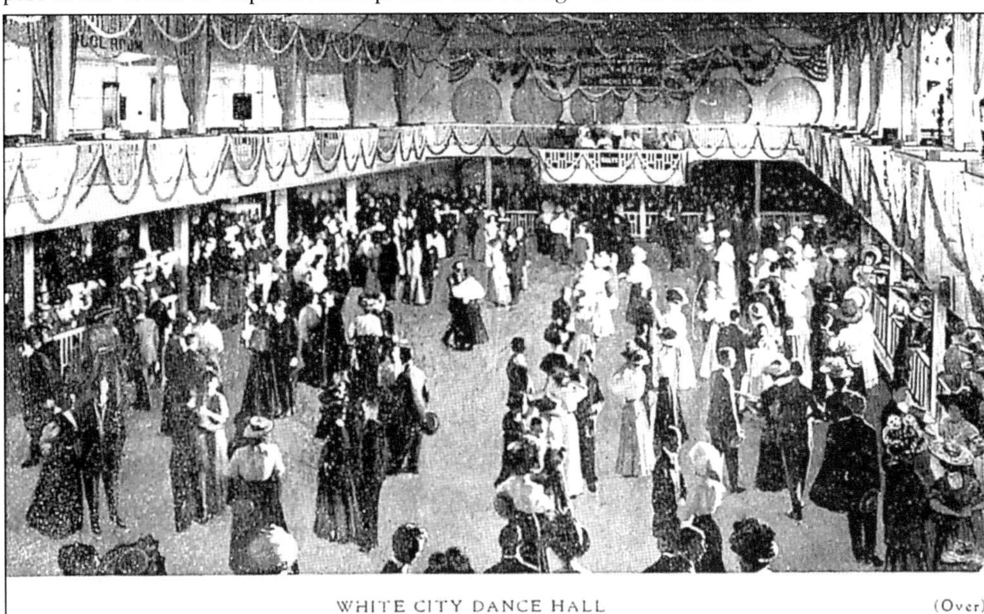

The White City dance hall was known by various names over the years. It began simply as White City dance hall, later was known as Danny Duggan's Deck, and still later was called the Spanish Villa. Dance marathons became a nationwide craze and several were held at White City. One woman who grew up near the park remembers the tired dancers getting a rest break and going for short walks up Route 9 before returning to the "dance grind." (Courtesy Erik Larson.)

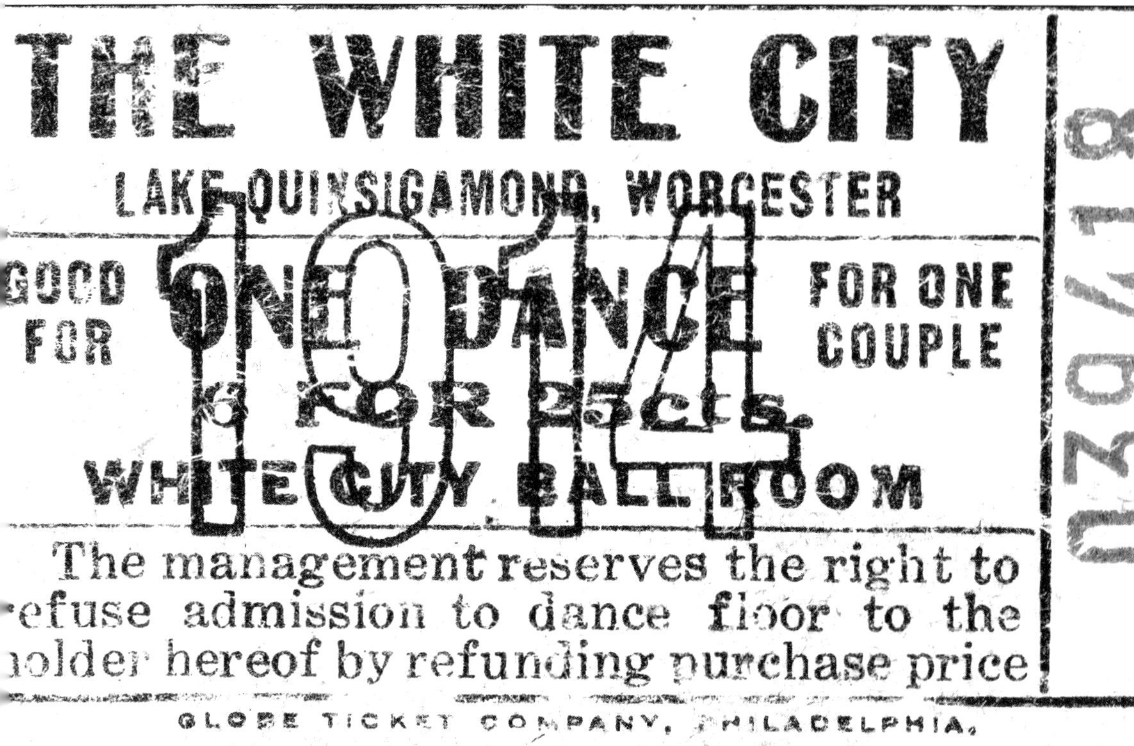

As late as 1914, White City Amusement Park was still advertised as being in Worcester, even though it was located across the lake in Shrewsbury, Massachusetts. At the time, Shrewsbury was a small village and not well known as a resort. Any printed matter, as well as many souvenir items, reflected the Worcester address for the park. This ticket for the White City Ball Room, for example, was bought during the 1914 season. In the 1990s, the ticket was discovered right where its owner had put it many years ago—in the shed of her home located in the neighborhood near the park.

The Mrs. Massachusetts pageant was held at White City in 1950. Here a few contestants pose for the camera (and an interested onlooker) aboard the carousel. Pictures of the White City carousel are very rare, although thousands of people must have taken photographs of friends riding on it over the years. (From the collections of the Worcester Historical Museum.)

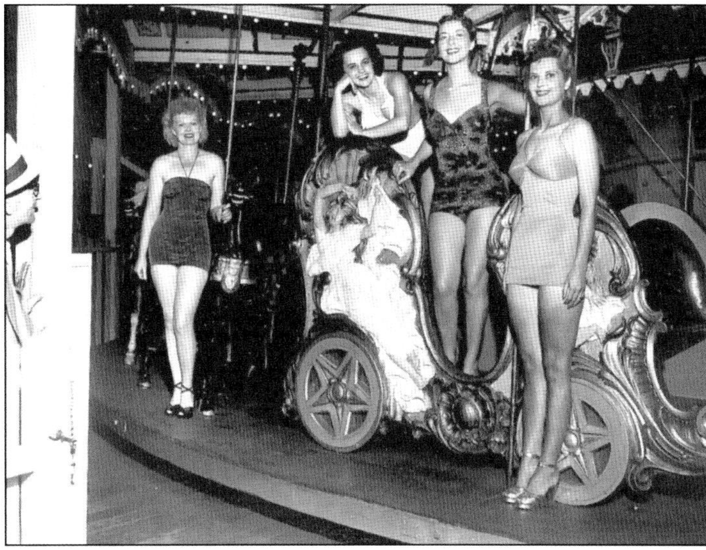

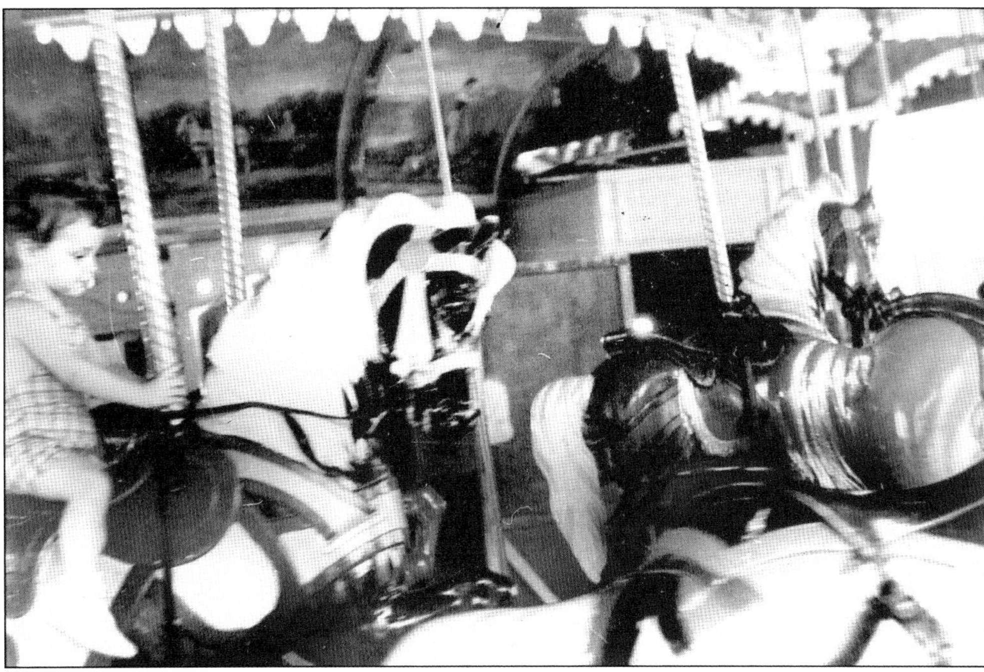

Entitled "Sherrie Rides the Horsie," this photograph shows Sherrie Krafve riding on the White City carousel c. 1955. This was the second carousel used at White City; it replaced an earlier ride in 1928. When the park closed, the carousel was auctioned off and moved to Oklahoma City. From there, it was sold again and relocated to Panama City, Florida. Known as PTC (Philadelphia Toboggan Company) No. 59, the carousel was auctioned off one horse or figure at a time after the Florida amusement park closed in the mid-1980s. The ride's superstructure and machinery were rediscovered in the 1990s. The Carousel Center in Pennsylvania purchased the remains of No. 59, refurbished the carousel with new hand-carved figures, and put it back in operation. Today, visitors to the park in Pennsylvania can once again experience the magic of riding on the White City carousel. (Courtesy Krafve family.)

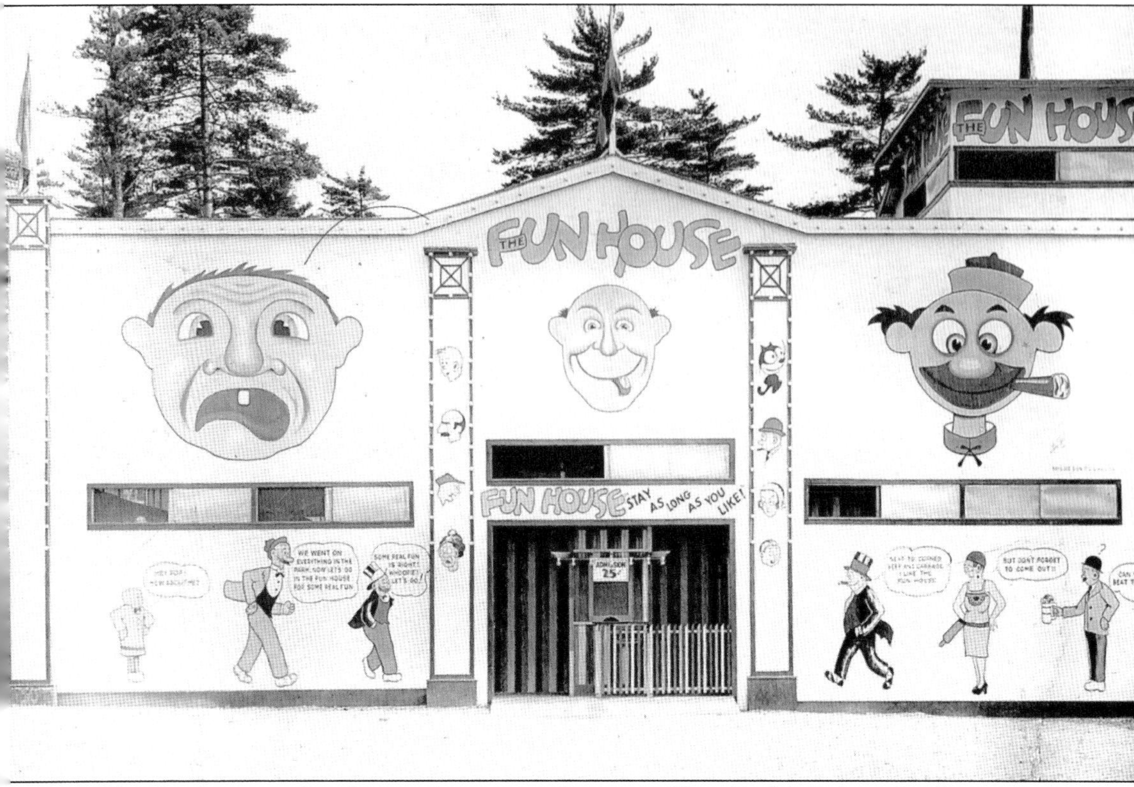

This fun house replaced an earlier version known as King Dodo's Palace. Inside was a steep slide, where riders would plummet over several dips while sitting on a ragbag. Other popular attractions inside included the Wheel of Fun, where the ride operator made a large wooden wheel spin faster and faster, until riders would start flying off; and the Barrel, which would tumble all but the most agile occupants. The final version of the fun house was designed with a medieval castle theme. The fun house was destroyed in one of a series of fires that plagued the park after it closed in 1960. (Courtesy John Richardson.)

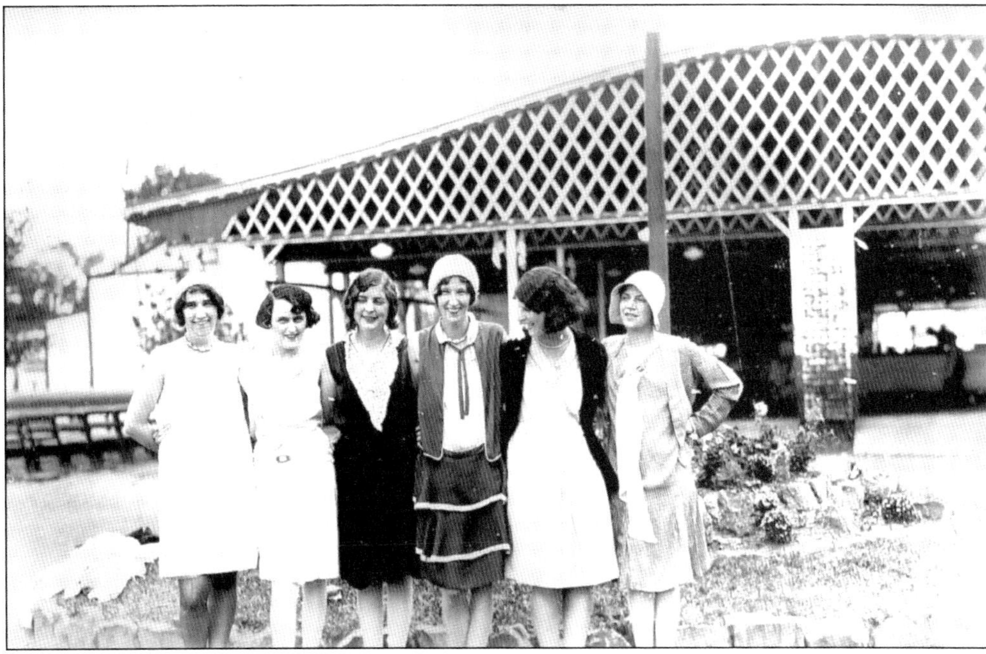

This photograph shows a group of young ladies out for a day of fun at White City c. 1928. The ride in the background is the Dodgem Cars, a feature of the park right up until it closed. Paul DiCicco, who worked on the ride as a teenager, recalls being shocked by the electric current that ran from a chicken-wire ceiling through a pole to power the cars. "OSHA would never allow this ride to operate in this day and age!" he related in a 2004 interview.

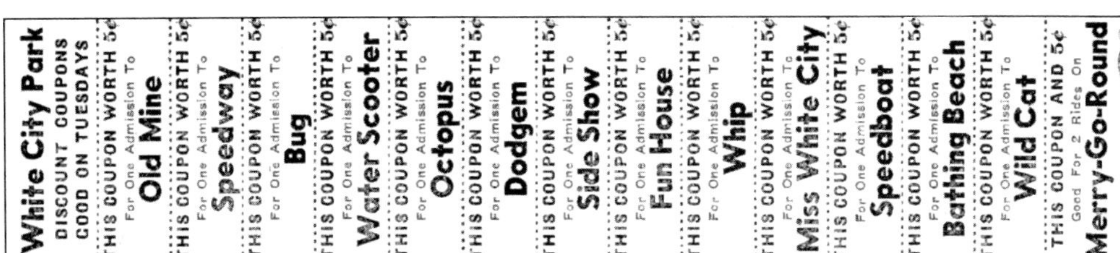

This strip of discount tickets could be used on Tuesdays at White City Park. Each ticket was good for one admission or ride on one of the various attractions at the park. The one exception was the ticket for the carousel, or Merry-Go-Round, which entitled the bearer to two rides. The wide variety of activities available for a day's fun is evident from these tickets. They represent only some of the many rides, games, and other attractions at the park.

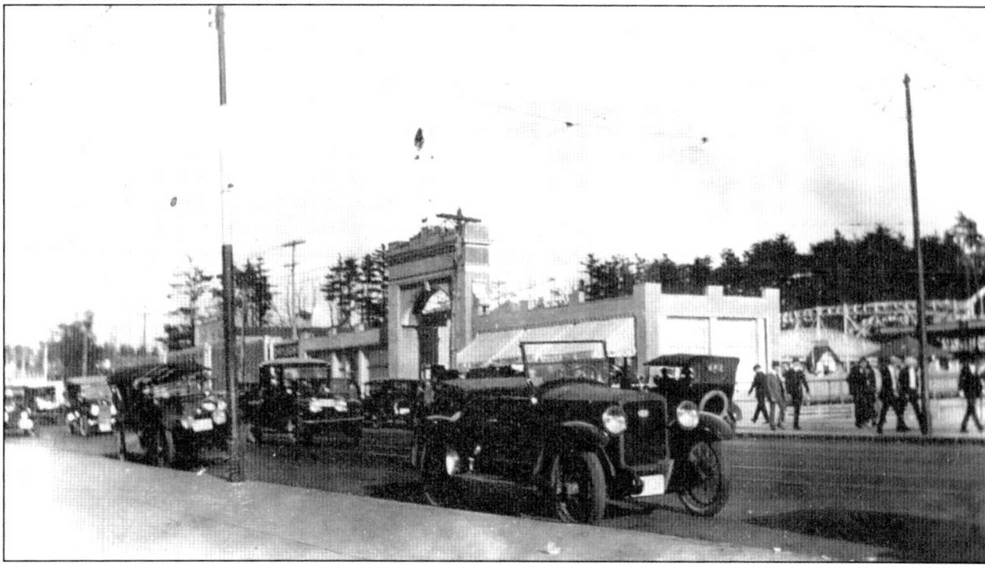

The main entrance to White City was originally built facing the Boston-Worcester Turnpike. As automobiles became the main means of transportation, parking lots were constructed at the rear of the park, with most people entering the park from that direction. This is how the Route 9 entrance appeared after the road had been modernized in the early 1930s. The roller coaster is just visible in the background. (Courtesy Erik Larson.)

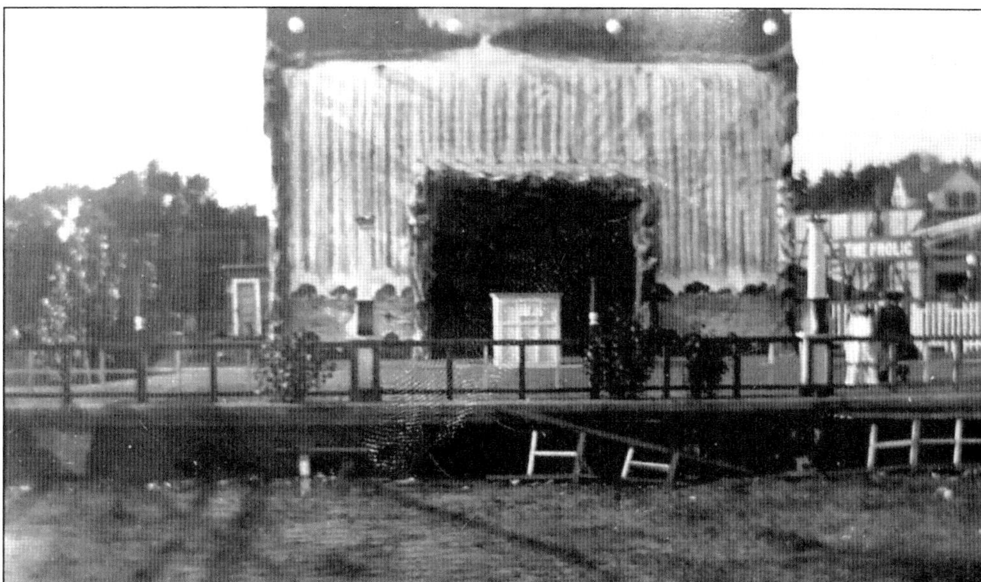

Over the course of White City's existence, many famous (and not-so-famous) acts appeared on the stage at the park. The acts were brought in to attract more customers, of course, and were for the most part very successful. The stage acts played a big part in the effort to revive interest in the park during the 1950s. Some of the well-known acts that appeared there included Bobby Darrin, Sandra Dee, the Four Aces, and the Four Coins, to name a few. Here the stage is shown in a *c.* 1930 photograph. (Courtesy John Richardson.)

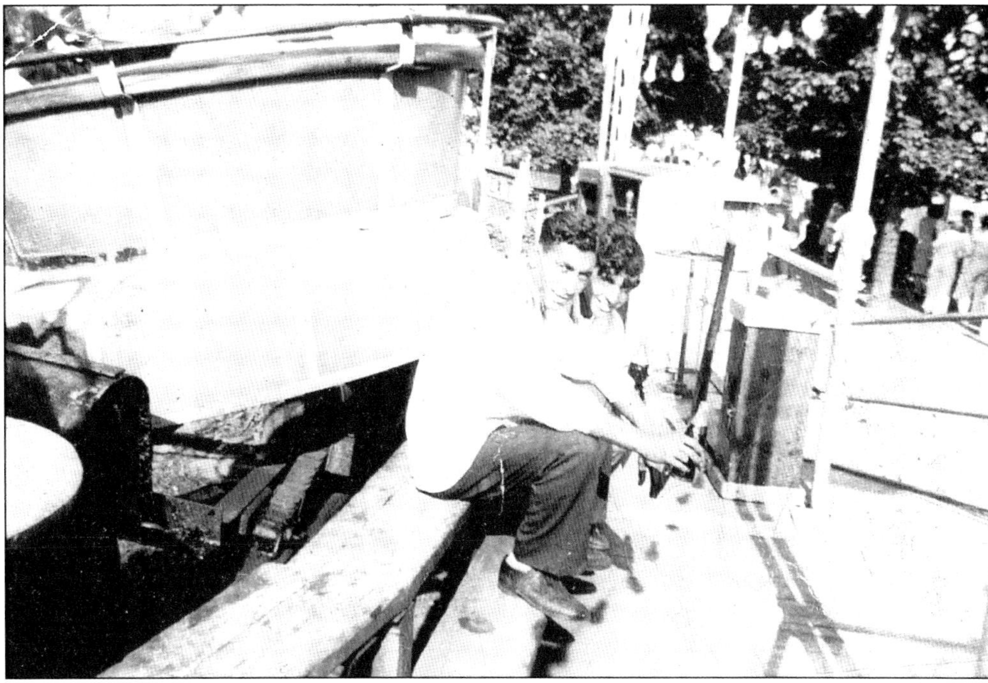

The Bug, one of many popular rides at White City Park, stands at the ready, waiting for some passengers to board. Michael Vuona, who worked at the park right up until the time it closed, is sitting on the step along with a friend. Michael and his wife, Lucy "Sally" Vuona, worked at the park for years, getting to know many of the visiting entertainers. It was not unusual for the Vuona household to host guests such as Emmett Kelly for a Sunday dinner of macaroni. (Courtesy Dorothy Vuona Skiest.)

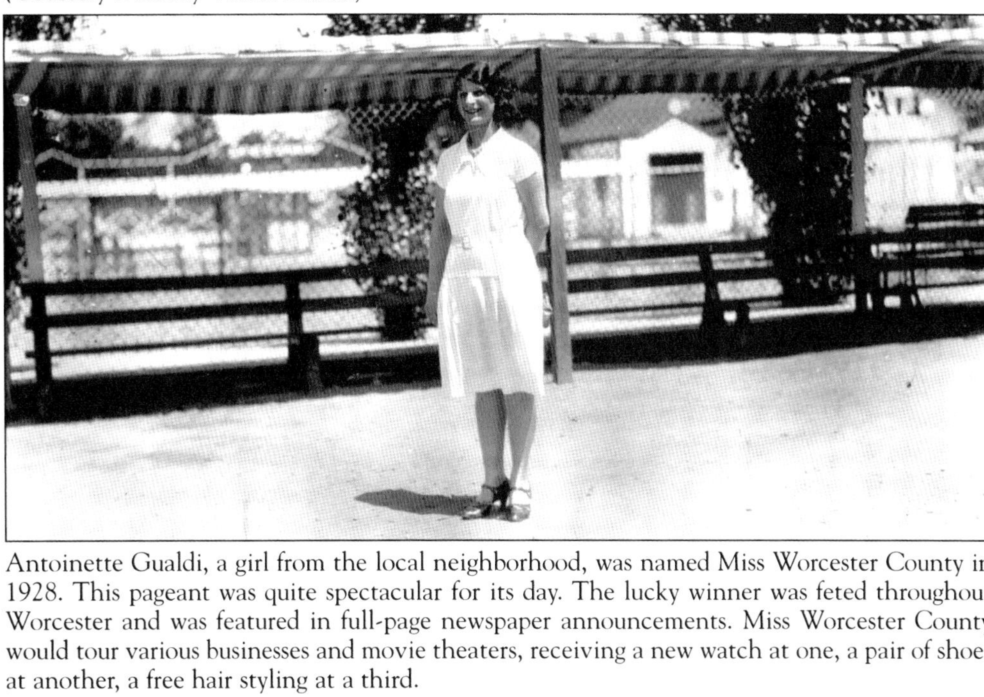

Antoinette Gualdi, a girl from the local neighborhood, was named Miss Worcester County in 1928. This pageant was quite spectacular for its day. The lucky winner was feted throughout Worcester and was featured in full-page newspaper announcements. Miss Worcester County would tour various businesses and movie theaters, receiving a new watch at one, a pair of shoes at another, a free hair styling at a third.

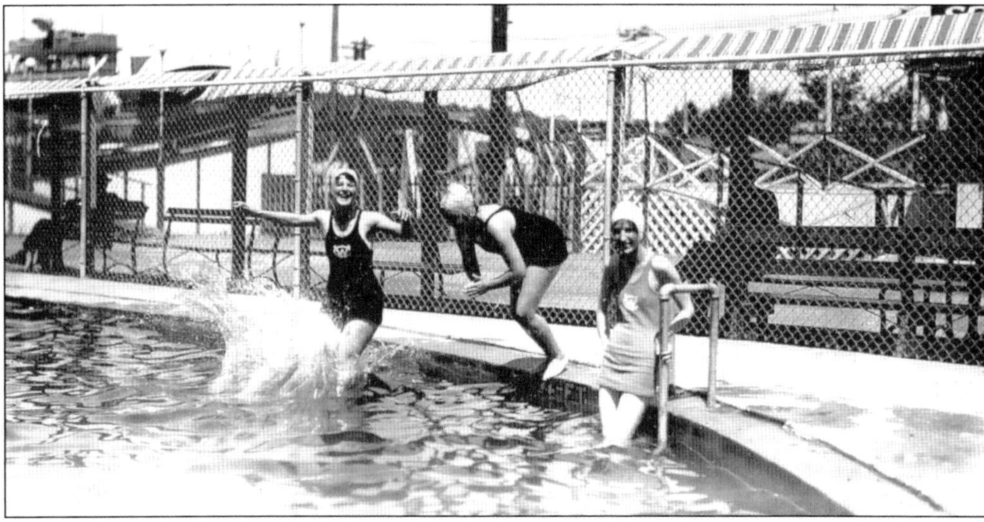

In the 1920s, the Shoot the Chutes ride was removed as part of an overall revamping of the park. The man-made pool that had been used as part of the ride was turned into a swimming pool. Bathing suits with "WC" imprinted on them (for White City) could be rented. Shown here are three young ladies, sporting those very suits, taking a dip in the new pool.

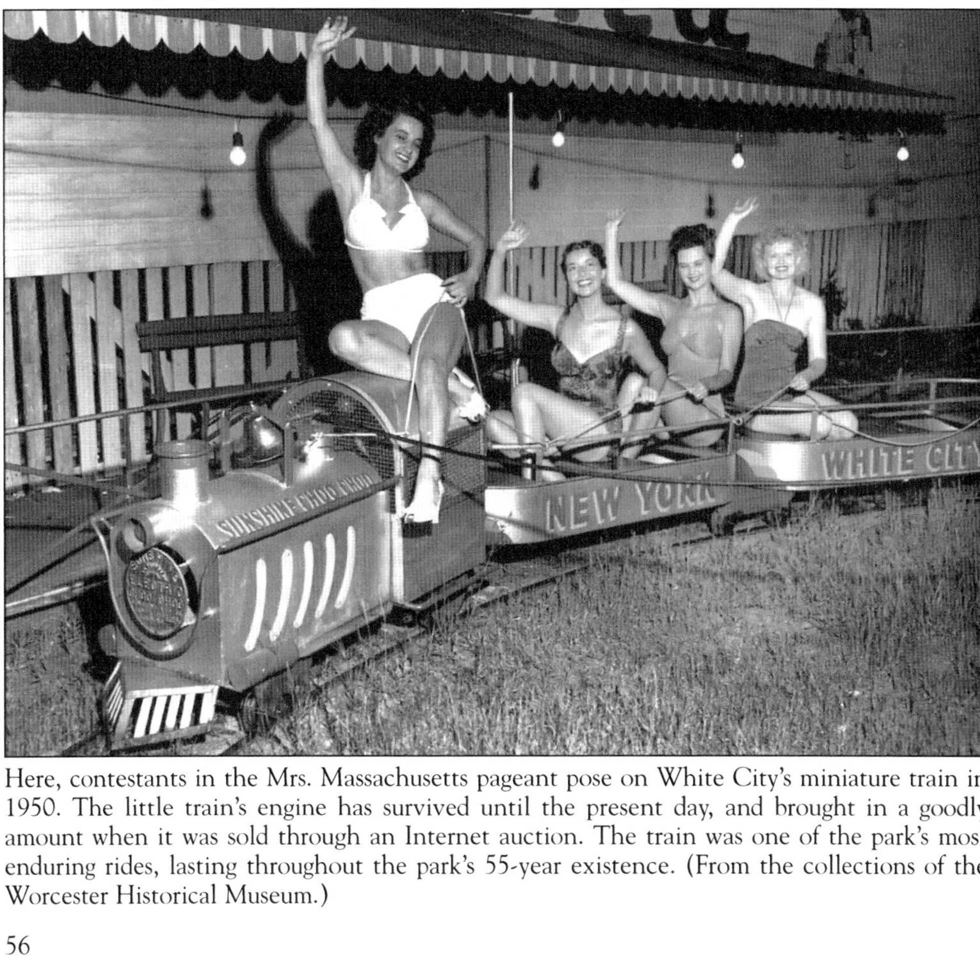

Here, contestants in the Mrs. Massachusetts pageant pose on White City's miniature train in 1950. The little train's engine has survived until the present day, and brought in a goodly amount when it was sold through an Internet auction. The train was one of the park's most enduring rides, lasting throughout the park's 55-year existence. (From the collections of the Worcester Historical Museum.)

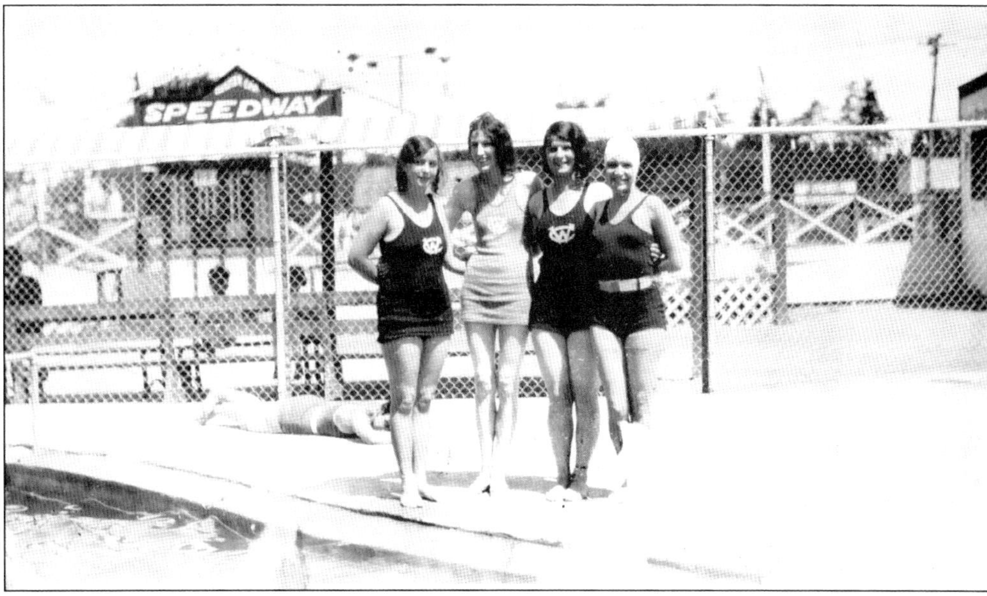

This photograph shows another group of bathing beauties at the White City pool. Some of these women were contestants in the Miss Worcester County beauty pageant in 1928. A sunbather, wearing the type of bathing suit that was in style at the time, can be seen reclining on the left.

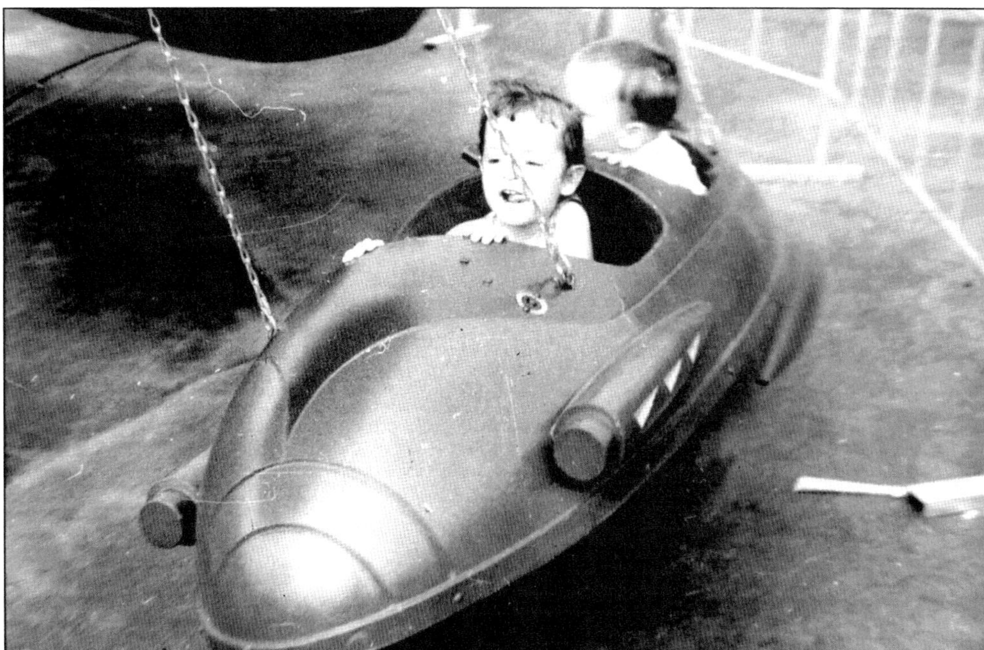
This photograph shows young Sherrie Krafve riding on a spaceship ride in Kiddieland, on July 2, 1955. Children made up a large part of White City's customers in its later years. One of the big attractions was an antique fire truck used to give the children rides around the park. The truck is still in the local area, and is owned by a man who grew up close to the park. (Courtesy Krafve Family.)

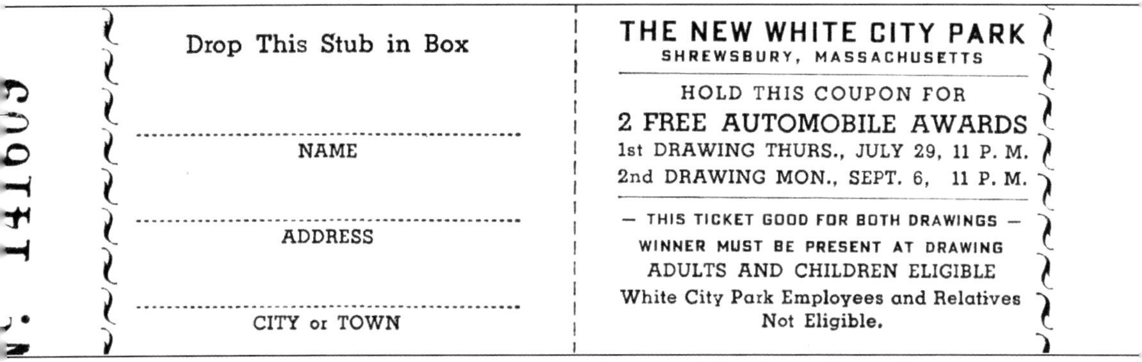

Drop This Stub in Box

NAME

ADDRESS

CITY or TOWN

THE NEW WHITE CITY PARK
SHREWSBURY, MASSACHUSETTS

HOLD THIS COUPON FOR
2 FREE AUTOMOBILE AWARDS
1st DRAWING THURS., JULY 29, 11 P. M.
2nd DRAWING MON., SEPT. 6, 11 P. M.

— THIS TICKET GOOD FOR BOTH DRAWINGS —
WINNER MUST BE PRESENT AT DRAWING
ADULTS AND CHILDREN ELIGIBLE
White City Park Employees and Relatives Not Eligible.

White City Amusement Park was bought by the Knohl family in the mid-1950s. The new owners made attempts to modernize the park to attract more business, billing the park as "The New White City Park." Well-known performers appeared at the park and new rides were added. An attempt to build a new roller coaster ended in disaster when a severe winter storm turned the partly completed ride into a heap of rubble. Contests to win new automobiles were another means of attracting customers, as shown on this ticket. It is interesting to note that the ticket states "Adults and Children Eligible." In the end, all of these efforts were unsuccessful in revitalizing White City. The park was seized for non-payment of taxes and closed on Labor Day 1960.

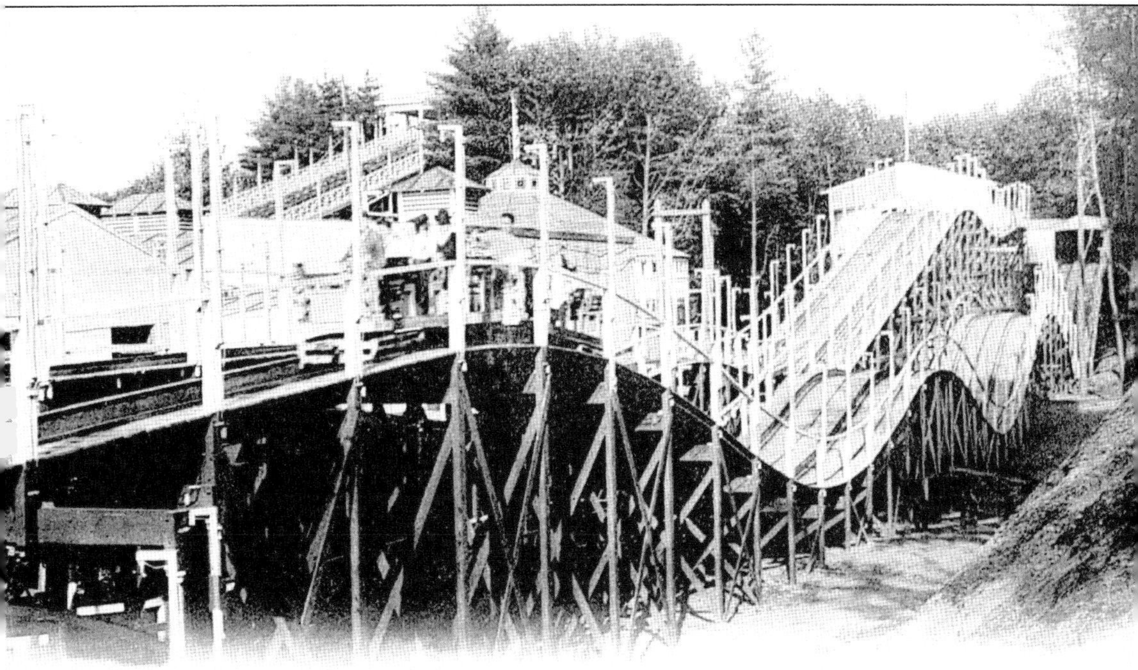

The roller coaster at White City Park was one of the most exciting rides to be found! Built by the Philadelphia Toboggan Company, the Zip had one vertical drop of 90 feet. Installed in the 1920s, the Zip replaced the earlier Scenic Railway, a view of which is shown in this postcard photo. Each spring, when the park was being readied for the coming summer season, the rides had to be tested out. Neighborhood children were delighted to be recruited to ride the coaster over and over, so that the weight of cars and passengers would wear away any rust on the tracks. Plans to replace the Zip fell through when a severe winter storm destroyed the new coaster, which was only partially completed, in 1956.

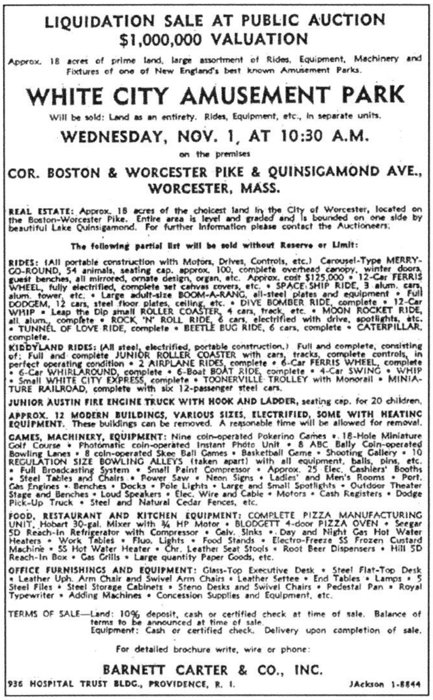

LIQUIDATION SALE AT PUBLIC AUCTION
$1,000,000 VALUATION

Approx. 18 acres of prime land, large assortment of Rides, Equipment, Machinery and Fixtures of one of New England's best known Amusement Parks.

WHITE CITY AMUSEMENT PARK

Will be sold: Land as an entirety. Rides, Equipment, etc., in separate units.

WEDNESDAY, NOV. 1, AT 10:30 A.M.

on the premises

COR. BOSTON & WORCESTER PIKE & QUINSIGAMOND AVE., WORCESTER, MASS.

REAL ESTATE: Approx. 18 acres of the choicest land in the City of Worcester, located on the Boston-Worcester Pike. Entire area is level and graded and is bounded on one side by beautiful Lake Quinsigamond. For further information please contact the Auctioneers.

The following partial list will be sold without Reserve or Limit:

RIDES: (All portable construction with Motors, Drives, Controls, etc.) Carousel-Type MERRY-GO-ROUND, 54 animals, seating cap. approx. 100, complete overhead canopy, winter doors, guest benches, all mirrored, ornate design, organ, etc. Approx. cost $125,000 • 12-Car FERRIS WHEEL, fully electrified, complete set canvas covers, etc. • SPACE SHIP RIDE, 3 alum. cars, alum. tower, etc. • Large adult-size BOOM-A-RANG, all-steel plates and equipment • Full DODGEM, 12 cars, steel floor plates, ceiling, etc. • DIVE BOMBER RIDE, complete • 12-Car WHIP • Leap the Dip small ROLLER COASTER, 4 cars, track, etc. • MOON ROCKET RIDE, all alum., complete • ROCK 'N' ROLL RIDE, 6 cars, electrified with drive, spotlights, etc. • TUNNEL OF LOVE RIDE, complete • BEETLE BUG RIDE, 6 cars, complete • CATERPILLAR, complete.

KIDDYLAND RIDES: (All steel, electrified, portable construction.) Full and complete, consisting of: Full and complete JUNIOR ROLLER COASTER with cars, tracks, complete controls, in perfect operating condition • 2 AIRPLANE RIDES, complete • 6-Car FERRIS WHEEL, complete • 6-Car WHIRLAROUND, complete • 6-Boat BOAT RIDE, complete • 4-Car SWING • WHIP • Small WHITE CITY EXPRESS, complete • TOONERVILLE TROLLEY with Monorail • MINIATURE RAILROAD, complete with six 12-passenger steel cars.

JUNIOR AUSTIN FIRE ENGINE TRUCK WITH HOOK AND LADDER, seating cap. for 20 children.

APPROX. 12 MODERN BUILDINGS, VARIOUS SIZES, ELECTRIFIED, SOME WITH HEATING EQUIPMENT. These buildings can be removed. A reasonable time will be allowed for removal.

GAMES, MACHINERY, EQUIPMENT: Nine coin-operated Pokerino Games • 18-Hole Miniature Golf Course • Photomatic coin-operated Instant Photo Unit • 8 ABC Bally Coin-operated Bowling Lanes • 8 coin-operated Skee Ball Games • Basketball Game • Shooting Gallery • 10 REGULATION SIZE BOWLING ALLEYS (taken apart) with all equipment, balls, pins, etc. • Full Broadcasting System • Small Paint Compressor • Approx. 25 Elec. Cashiers' Booths • Steel Tables and Chairs • Power Saw • Neon Signs • Ladies' and Men's Rooms • Port. Gas Engines • Benches • Docks • Pole Lights • Large and Small Spotlights • Outdoor Theater Stage and Benches • Loud Speakers • Elec. Wire and Cable • Motors • Cash Registers • Dodge Pick-Up Truck • Steel and Natural Cedar Fences, etc.

FOOD, RESTAURANT AND KITCHEN EQUIPMENT: COMPLETE PIZZA MANUFACTURING UNIT, Hobart 30-gal. Mixer with ¾ HP Motor • BLODGETT 4-door PIZZA OVEN • Seegar 5D Reach-in Refrigerator with Compressor • Galv. Sinks • Day and Night Gas Hot Water Heaters • Work Tables • Fluo. Lights • Food Stands • Electro-Freeze SS Frozen Custard Machine • SS Hot Water Heater • Chr. Leather Seat Stools • Root Beer Dispensers • Hill 5D Reach-In Box • Gas Grills • Large quantity Paper Goods, etc.

OFFICE FURNISHINGS AND EQUIPMENT: Glass-Top Executive Desk • Steel Flat-Top Desk • Leather Uph. Arm Chair and Swivel Arm Chairs • Leather Settee • End Tables • Lamps • 5 Steel Files • Steel Storage Cabinets • Steno Desks and Swivel Chairs • Pedestal Pan • Royal Typewriter • Adding Machines • Concession Supplies and Equipment, etc.

TERMS OF SALE—Land: 10% deposit, cash or certified check at time of sale. Balance of terms to be announced at time of sale.
Equipment: Cash or certified check. Delivery upon completion of sale.

For detailed brochure write, wire or phone:

BARNETT CARTER & CO., INC.

936 HOSPITAL TRUST BLDG., PROVIDENCE, R. I. JAckson 1-8844

A year after White City Amusement Park closed, an auction was held to sell off all the park's rides, equipment, and land. White City, after a 55-year existence, was sold off piece by piece until nothing remained. According to one rumor, the Ferris wheel was rolled into Lake Quinsigamond. Once the amusement park was finally closed and dismantled, the White City shopping center was built on the former site of the park.

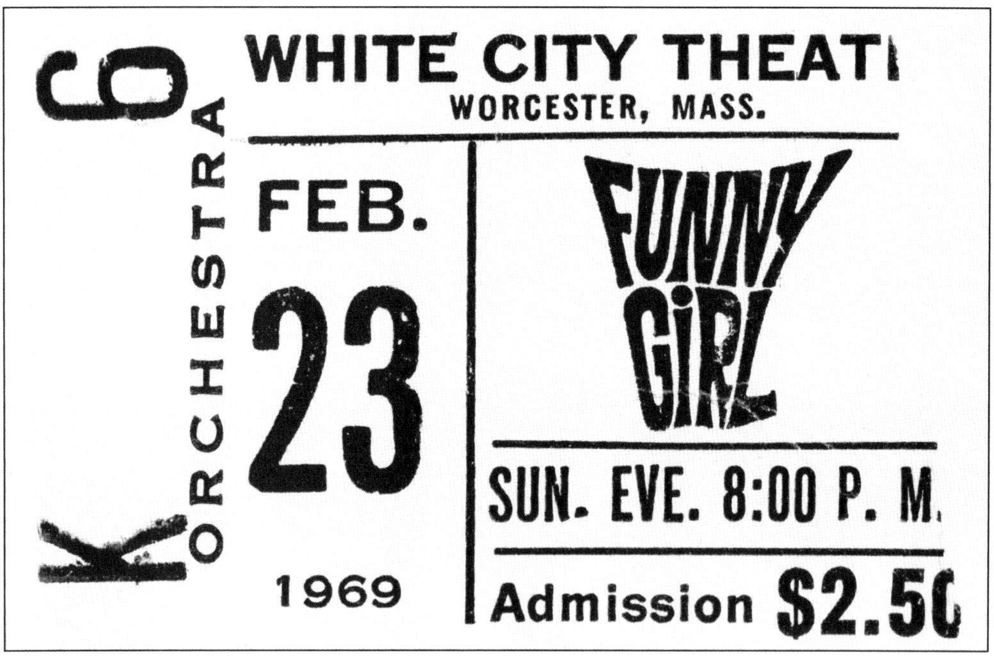

A latecomer to the scene, White City Cinemas opened for business in January 1965. The theater was said to be the first in Worcester County located in a shopping center. This ticket stub survived the Sunday evening showing of *Funny Girl* on February 23, 1969. The theater was eventually converted into a two-screen layout, and still later, a three-screen arrangement. But even this was not enough to keep up with the modern multiplex cinemas; White City Theater closed its doors forever in March 2001. A restaurant stands on the site today.

Three

Clubhouses, Hotels, and Beaches

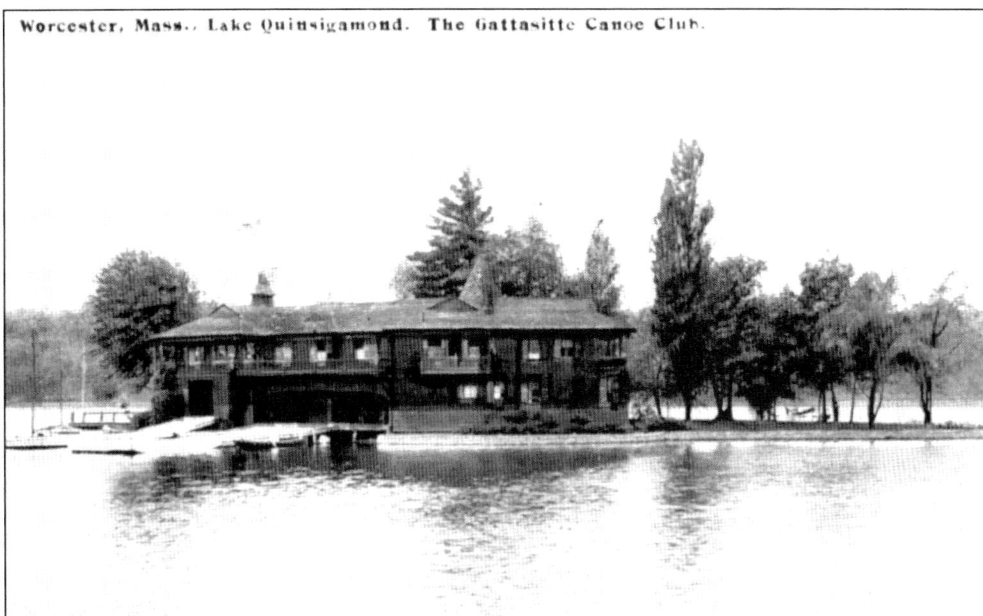

Formed in 1889, the Tatassit Canoe Club became one of the most active groups of many that had clubhouses on Lake Quinsigamond. Within two years, the Tatassits built a beautiful clubhouse on little Plum Island, which allowed quick access from the shore only a short distance away. The Tatassits became known for their production of stage shows, to say nothing of their large war canoe, in which they traveled up and down the lake. The club was active until the 1920s, when the property was turned into Tatassit Beach. Many postcard views of the Tatassit Canoe Club exist, including this one, on which the word Tatassit is misspelled as "Gattasitte."

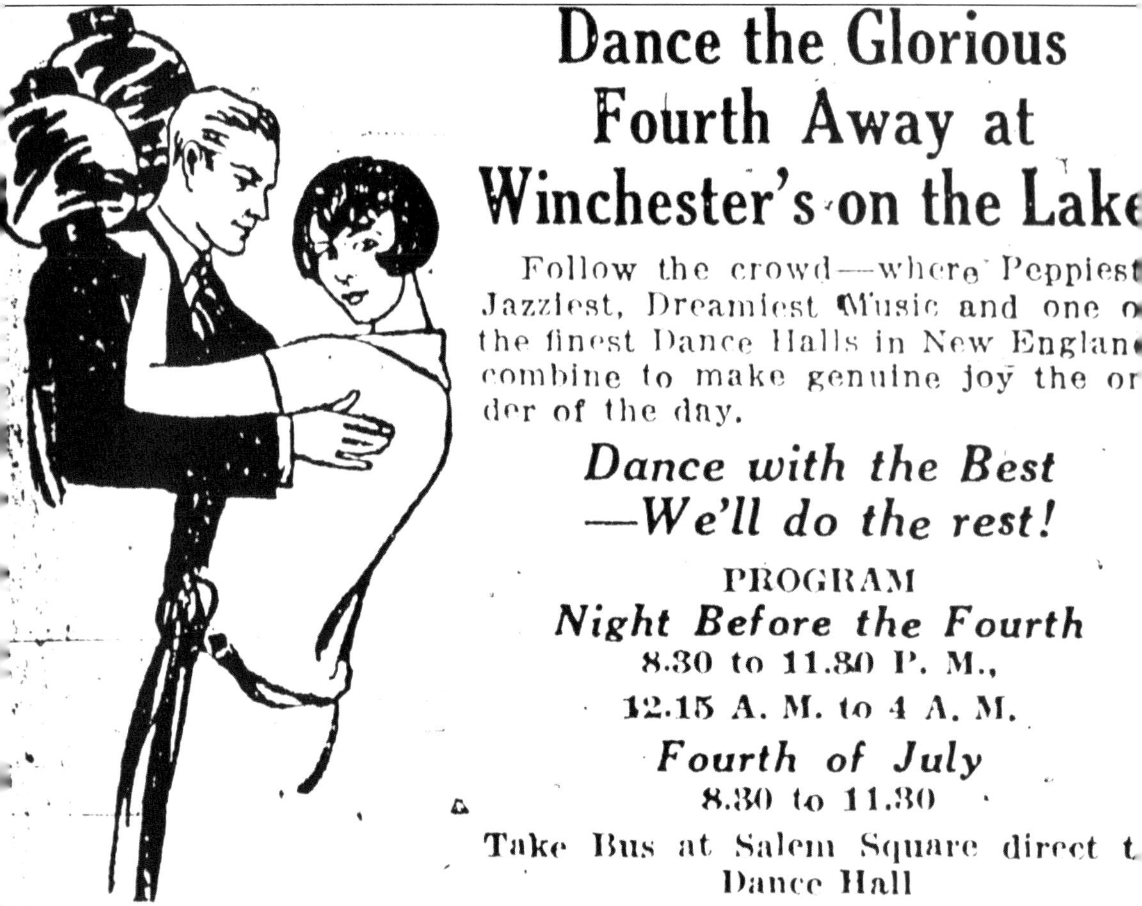

Winchester's on the Lake was one of a number of popular dance halls. It featured a dance floor and dining rooms, as well as picnic grounds. Located on Lake Avenue, the business started around 1910 and continued well into the 1940s. Winchester's was famous for its summer clambakes. Harry Winchester, the owner, was a well-known local sportsman. He also operated two boathouses on the lake.

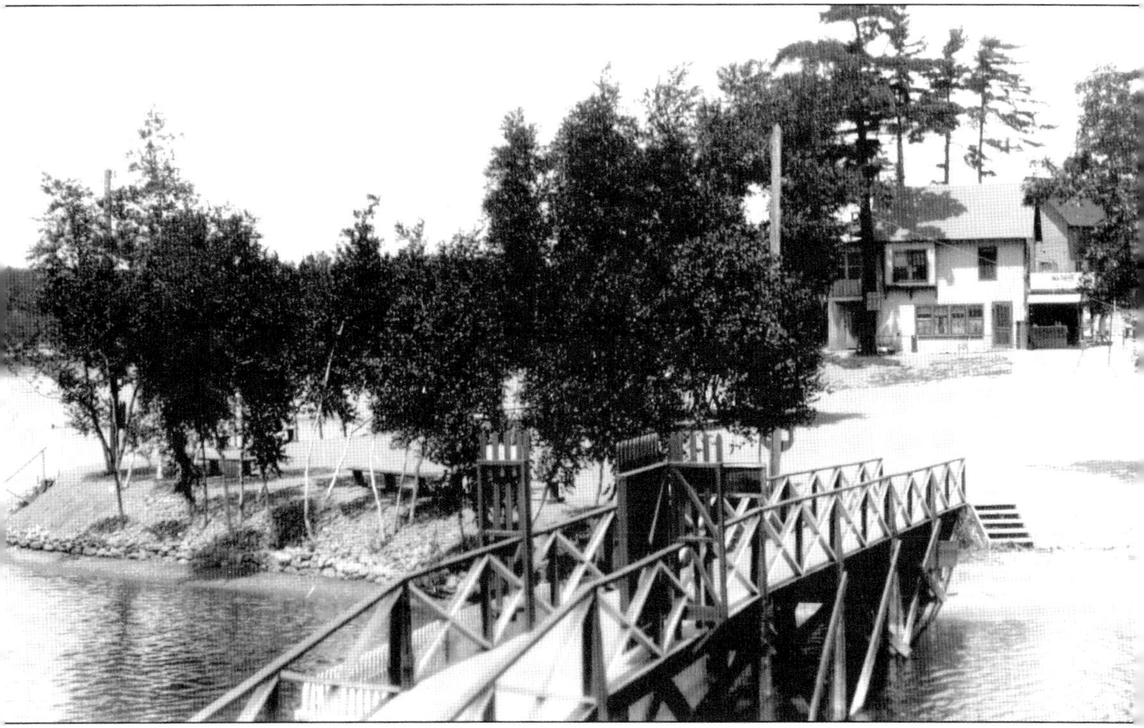

This little bridge was built to allow easier access to Tatassit Island, which was only accessible by boat before the bridge was constructed. This photograph of the bridge, as viewed while looking toward the shore, was likely taken from one of the porches of the building on the island. When activity was in full swing at the High Hat nightclub and restaurant, a tall man wearing a cape and top hat would greet visitors to the island by removing his hat, bowing, and saying "Welcome to the High Hat!" (Courtesy Judy Koffman.)

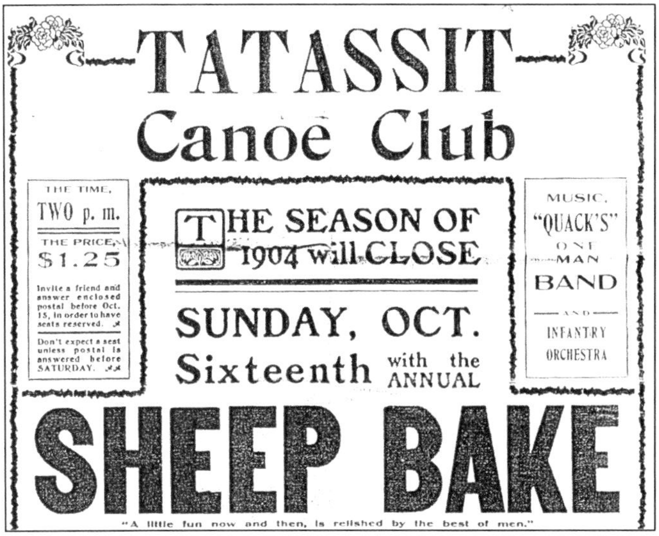

In 1904, the Tatassit Canoe Club closed its summer season with the 16th in a series of annual "sheep bakes." The sheep would be baked by "Uncle Andrew" Holt, a.k.a. "The Pride of Palmer." It was said, "There are other would-be sheep bakers, but none are in the same class with 'Uncle Andrew,' who has baked so many that he's ashamed to look a sheep in the face." As can be seen in the ad, music was provided by Quack's One Man Band and Infantry Orchestra.

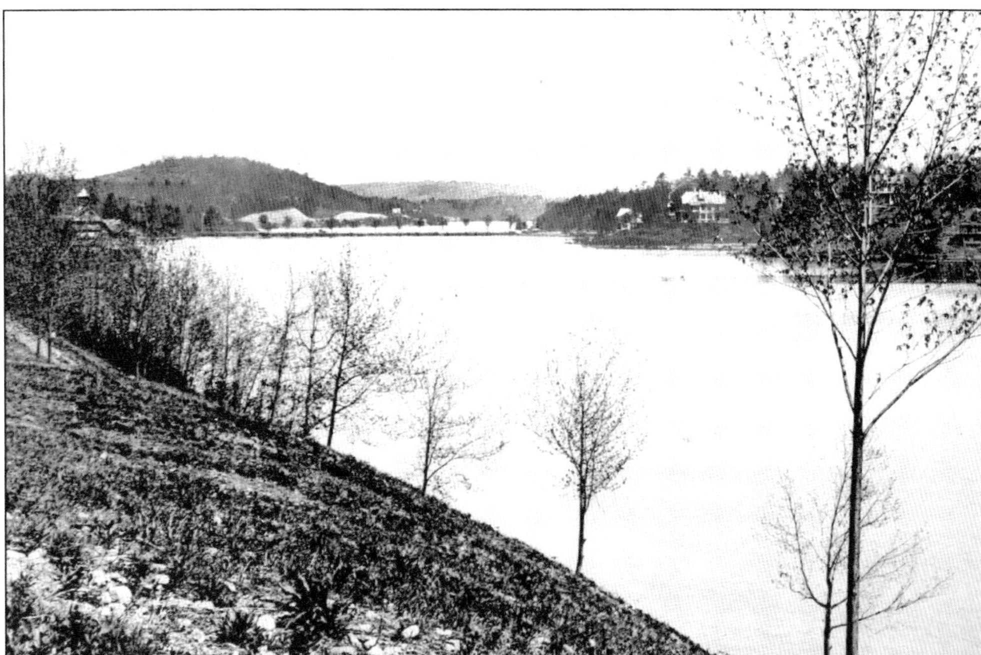

This photo-postcard image was taken from the top of the steep, sloping shoreline at what is now Quinsigamond State Park. As can be seen, the surrounding area was virtually devoid of structures at this time. The causeway is visible in the distance to the north. This area is heavily wooded today.

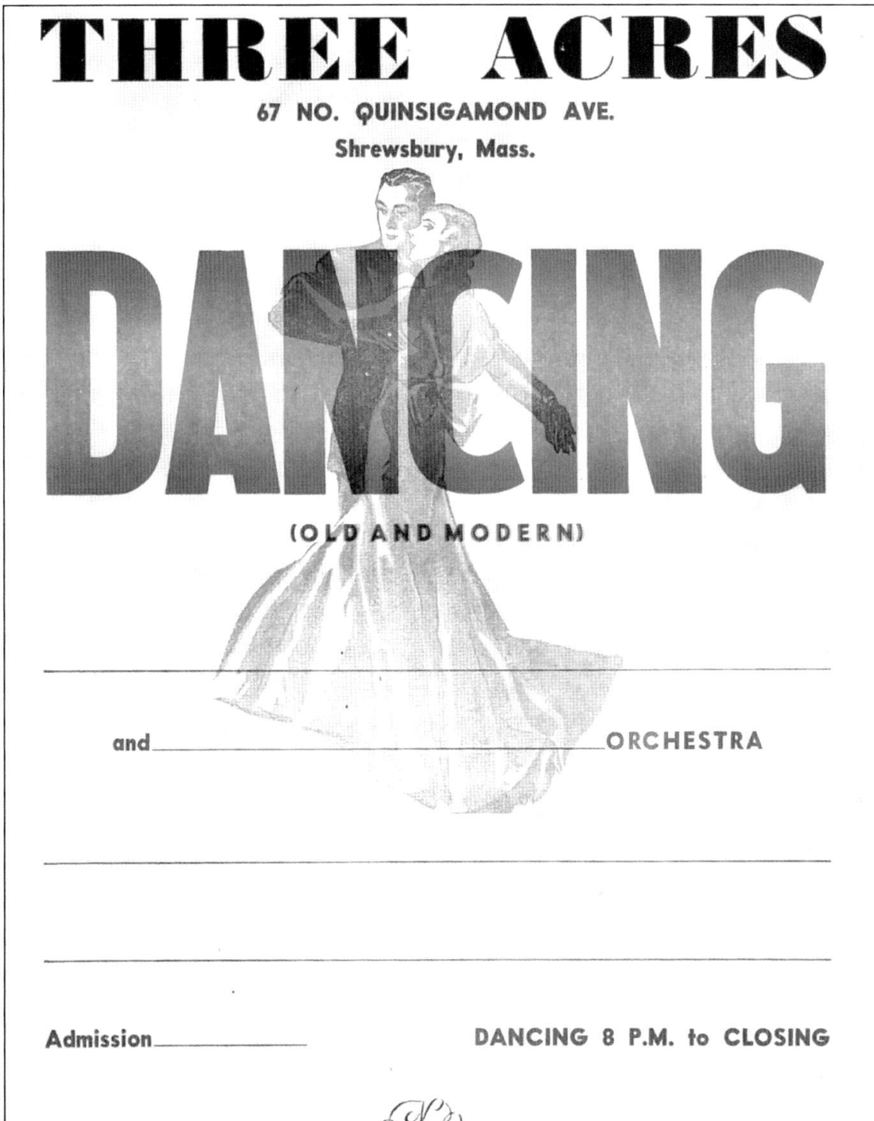

The Three Acres club was located on North Quinsigamond Avenue in Shrewsbury. The club was popular for dancing in the 1930s, as evidenced by the broadside shown here. Other popular dance halls included Winchester's on Lake Avenue, Olympia Park and Maironis Park on South Quinsigamond Avenue, and of course, the dance halls at Lincoln Park and White City. The Three Acres membership was made up of people of Finnish heritage. During World War II, rumors spread that Communist activities were taking place at the club, prompting town employees to be told to keep an eye on the place "on the q.t." As far as anyone knows, no illicit activities of any sort took place at the club. The Three Acres existed until recent years, when the property was sold, the building was torn down, and condominiums were built on the site.

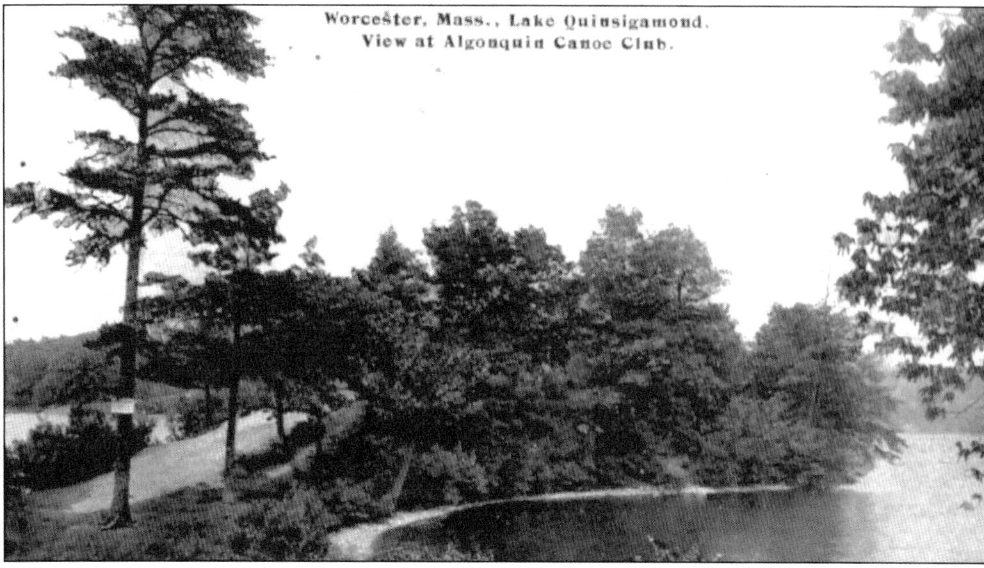

This peninsula juts out from the shore off Lake Avenue. It was originally home to the part of the Wapiti Club that stood on the shore, as opposed to the clubhouse on Wapiti Island. Later, the building on the peninsula became home to the Algonquin Canoe Club. Still later, it was known as the Bungalow, and finally, was the Lithuanian Naturalization and Social Club. The building was replaced in 1922; that structure burned down in 1930, and was replaced by another structure, which burned down in 1972. This location is now the site of a private home.

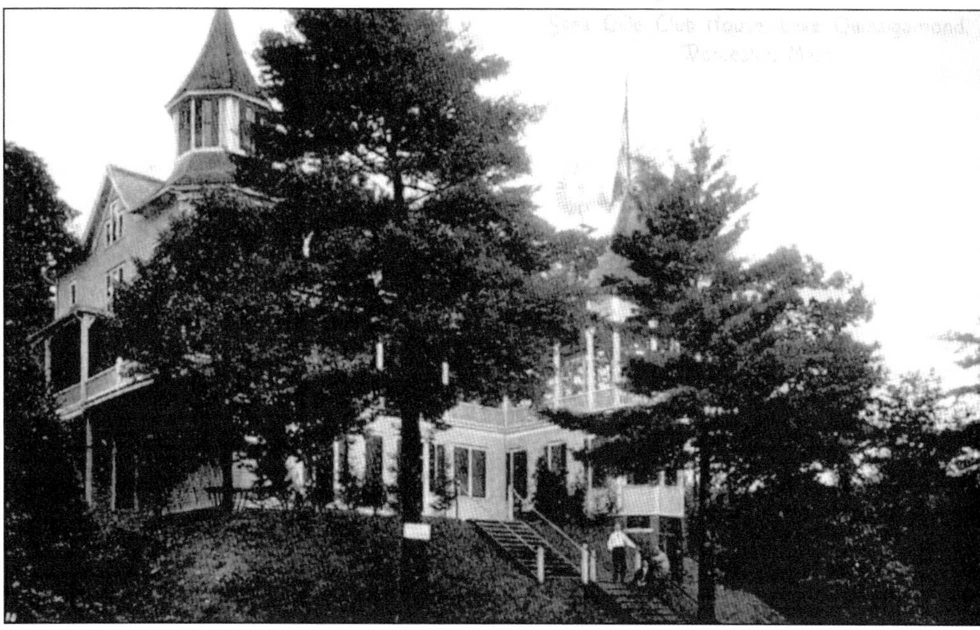

This clubhouse was located on 15 acres of land at what is now the intersection of Oak Street and South Quinsigamond Avenue. One of the largest clubhouses on the lake, it was an impressive structure. It was crowned by tall towers with flights of stairs leading down to the water. This Swedish ethnic club, Svea Gille, was popular into the 1950s, but was sold when interest waned in the 1960s. It was subsequently home to the Quinsigamond Athletic Club. The building was later razed, and condominiums stand on the site today.

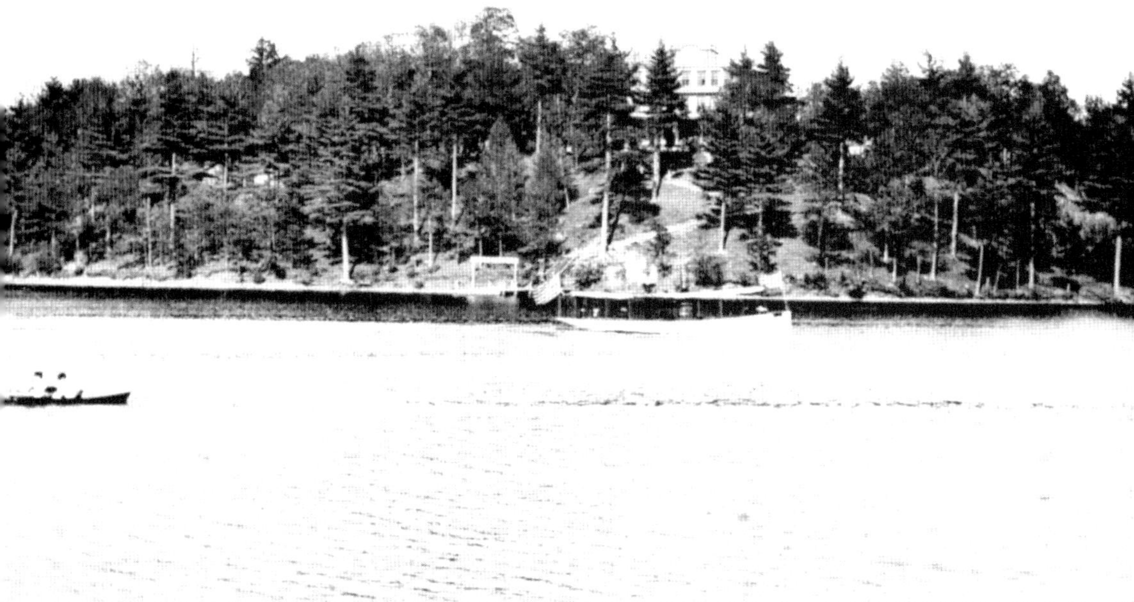

The Eyrie Hotel was one of a number of summer hotels on the lake. It was home to the elaborate Eyrie Gardens, a windmill, duck pond, and even a live eagle, which was fed by local boys who would catch fish for it. The dock at the hotel was one of the routine stops for the many steamboats that chugged up and down the lake, the primary means of reaching the site for many years. Eventually, a road was built that allowed carriages to get as far as the hotel. The Eyrie eventually turned into what was called Olympia Park, a well-known dance spot during the 1930s and 1940s. Later, Olympia Park was torn down, the hill was removed, and condominiums were built on the site, which is on South Quinsigamond Avenue, across from Ridgeland Road.

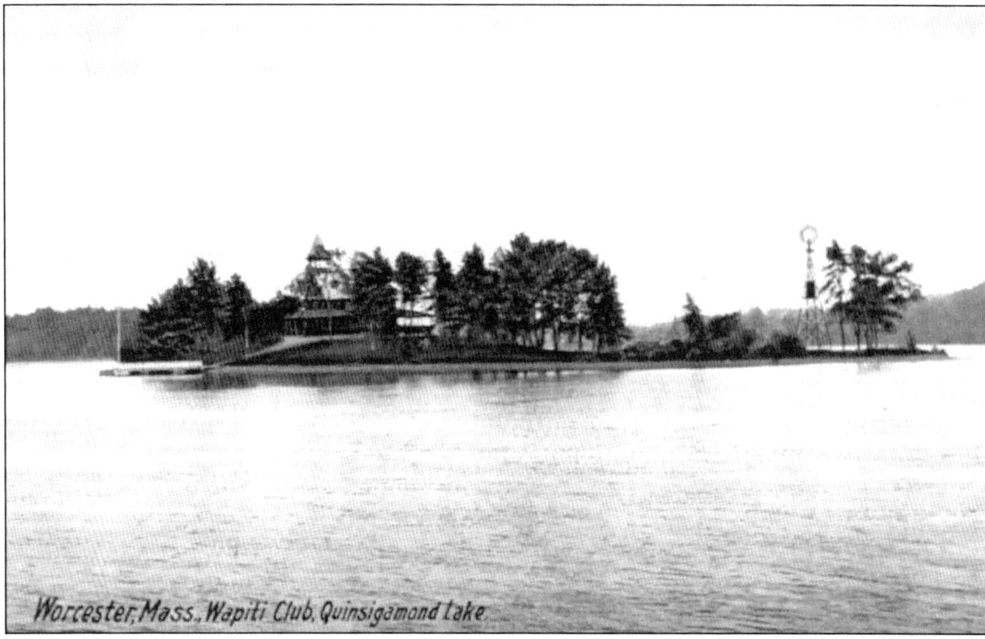

The Wapiti Club actually had two locations at Lake Quinsigamond, one on what became known as Wapiti Island (shown here), the other on the Worcester shore. The clubhouse on the island was very elaborate, according to contemporary accounts. The Wapitis were all members of the Elks. Unfortunately, the Wapiti Club's island retreat only lasted a very short time, as a huge fire in the winter of 1902 destroyed the building.

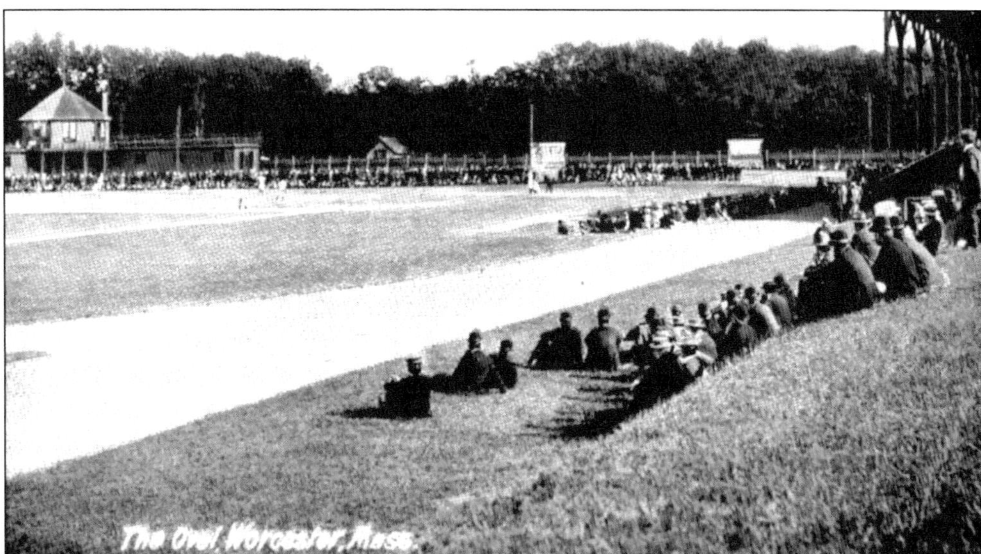

The Oval was another creation of H. H. Bigelow. Located in the Lake View area of Worcester, not far from what is now Quinsigamond State Park, the Oval was a combination ball field and arena. Elaborate productions were staged here, including one depicting scenes from ancient Rome! Many early baseball games were played at the Oval. The Oval was eventually closed and torn down.

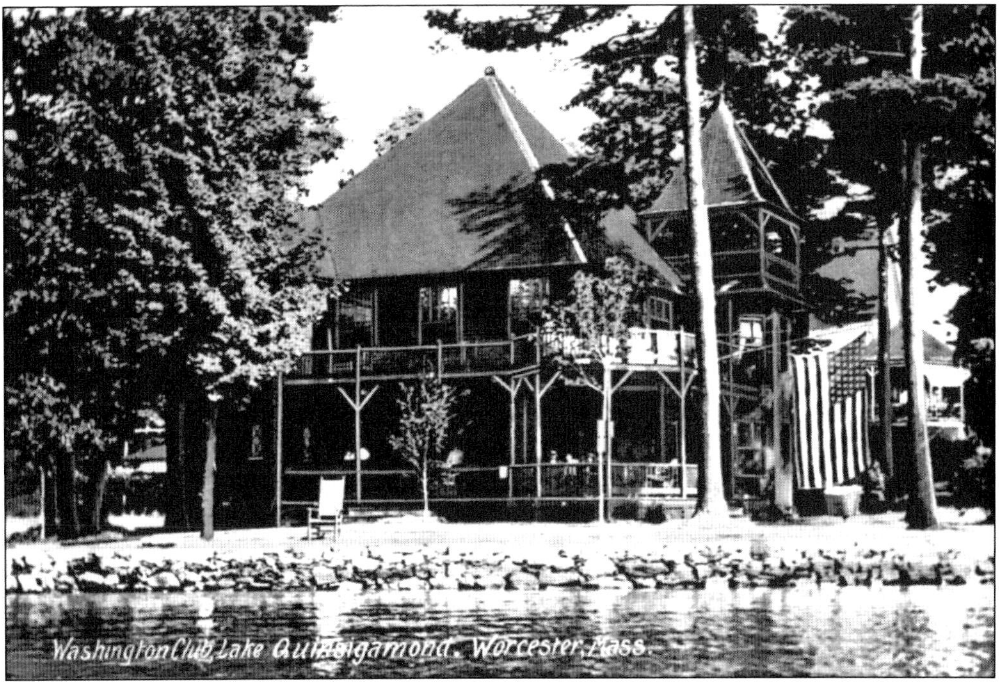

Built by an Irish social organization in 1887, the Washington Club was one of the largest and best-equipped clubhouses on Lake Quinsigamond. The club grounds included a baseball diamond and tennis courts. Boats and canoes were available for the use of members. The clubhouse itself burned during the early 1960s. A much smaller cement-block structure was erected and was used until the property was sold in 1996. A private home stands at this location today.

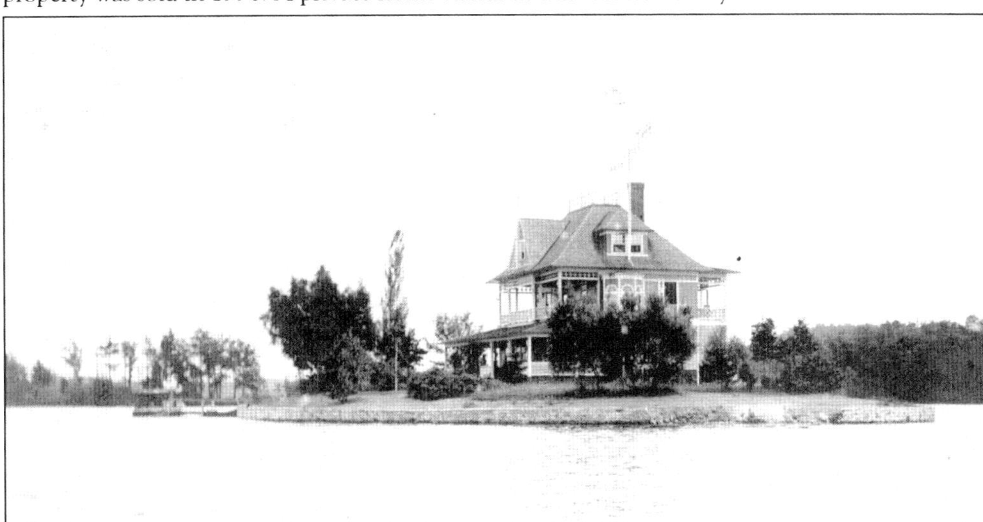

A French ethnic club called the Rostrevor Club occupied Sugarloaf Island. At other times, both the Frontenac Club and the Progress Club used the building. The Rostrevors were perhaps the best known of the three groups, because for many years the island was still known as Rostrevor's Island. The building was quite large for the available space on the island. Some accounts relate that when the club was first opened in the spring, the water level was so high that club members would get their feet wet walking from the dock to the clubhouse. (Courtesy Barton Kamp.)

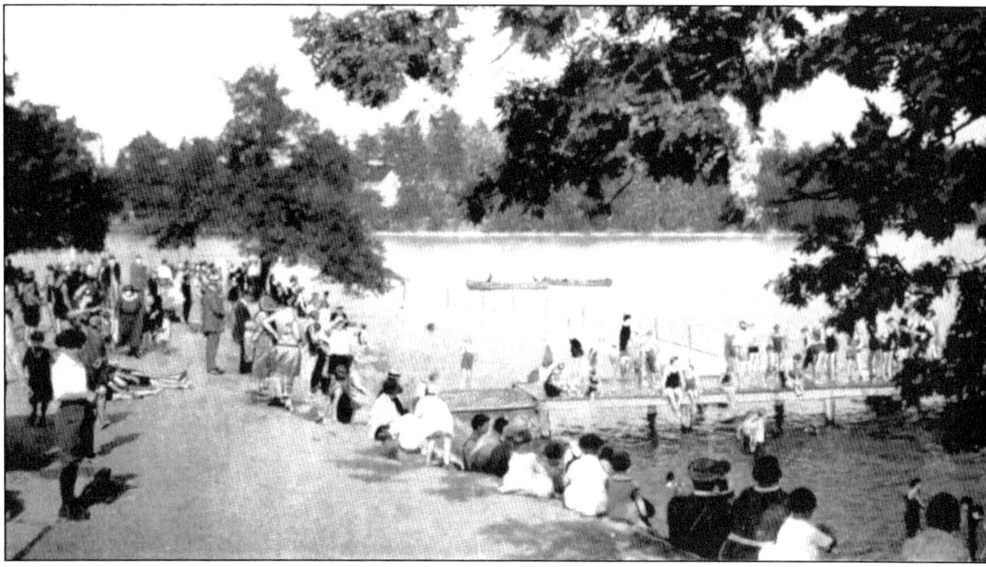

Quinsigamond State Park includes many acres of land. In the 1800s, the same area was untouched woodland. As the area around Lake Quinsigamond was developed into a pleasure resort, Horace H. Bigelow and Isaac Davis saw the potential for even more expansion. They gave a large tract of land to the city, and Quinsigamond Park was established there. The beach at Quinsigamond Park became a popular attraction. It is shown here hosting crowds of bathers c. 1907.

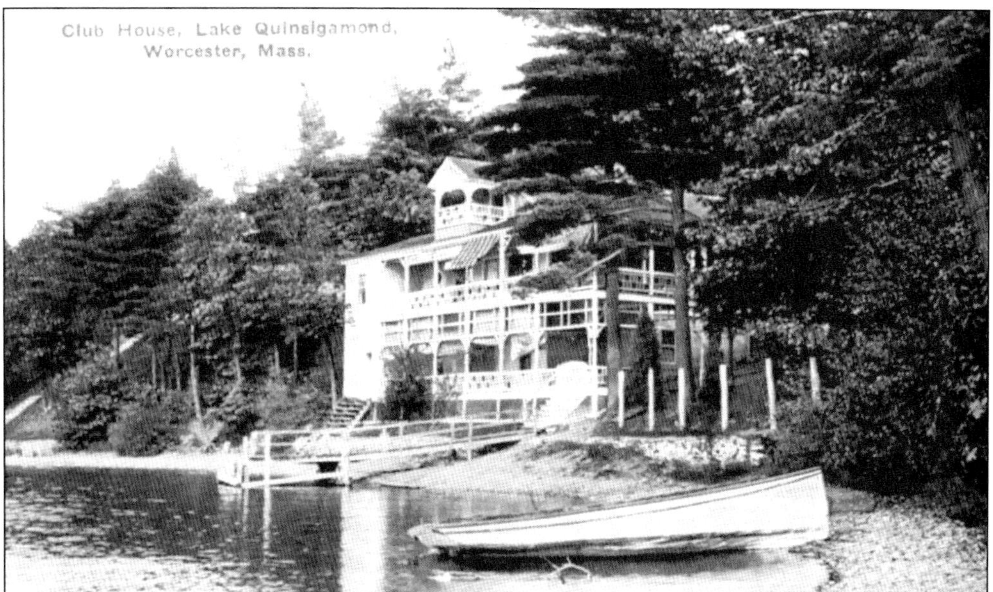

The Turner Club, sometimes known as the Social Turn Verein, was a group whose members were German. The focus of the club was physical fitness, and members were known for their amazing feats. Built in 1868, the building is one of the sole remnants of the glory days of Lake Quinsigamond. After the Turners, this structure was home to Groezingers restaurant and ice cream parlor, and then was the Lakeman's Lodge for a short time. The Lithuanian War Veterans purchased the property more than 50 years ago. In 2004, it again changed hands and is now owned by the Knights of Columbus.

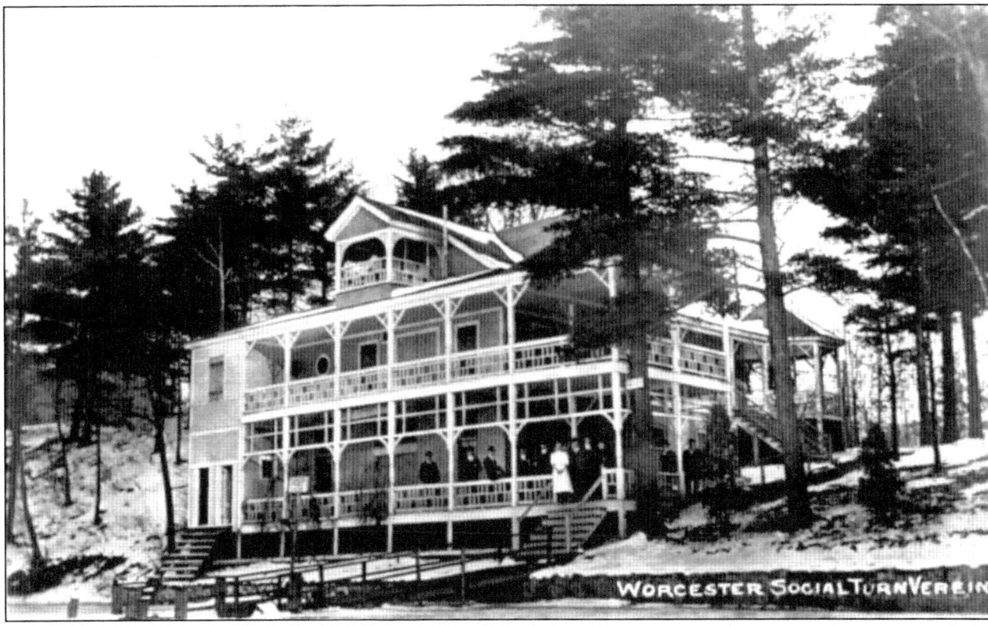

This postcard shows the Turner Club in a rare scene with snow on the ground. Very few Lake Quinsigamond views were photographed in winter, as there was little going on during the winter months. As summer approached, the clubs would have a gala opening period, usually around Memorial Day, with various activities and festivities. (Courtesy Barton Kamp.)

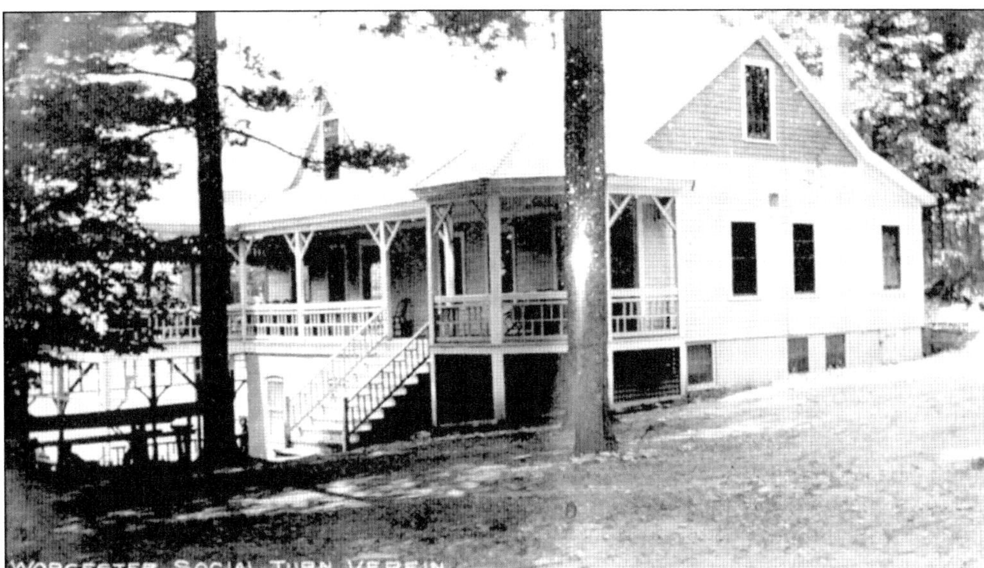

Here is an image of the Turner Club, viewed from what is now South Quinsigamond Avenue toward the lake. This picture provides a unique perspective since most photographs of the Turner Club were taken from the lake side, looking toward the shore. With some updates over the years, this building still looks very similar to its original configuration. The area in the immediate foreground is now a parking lot. (Courtesy Barton Kamp.)

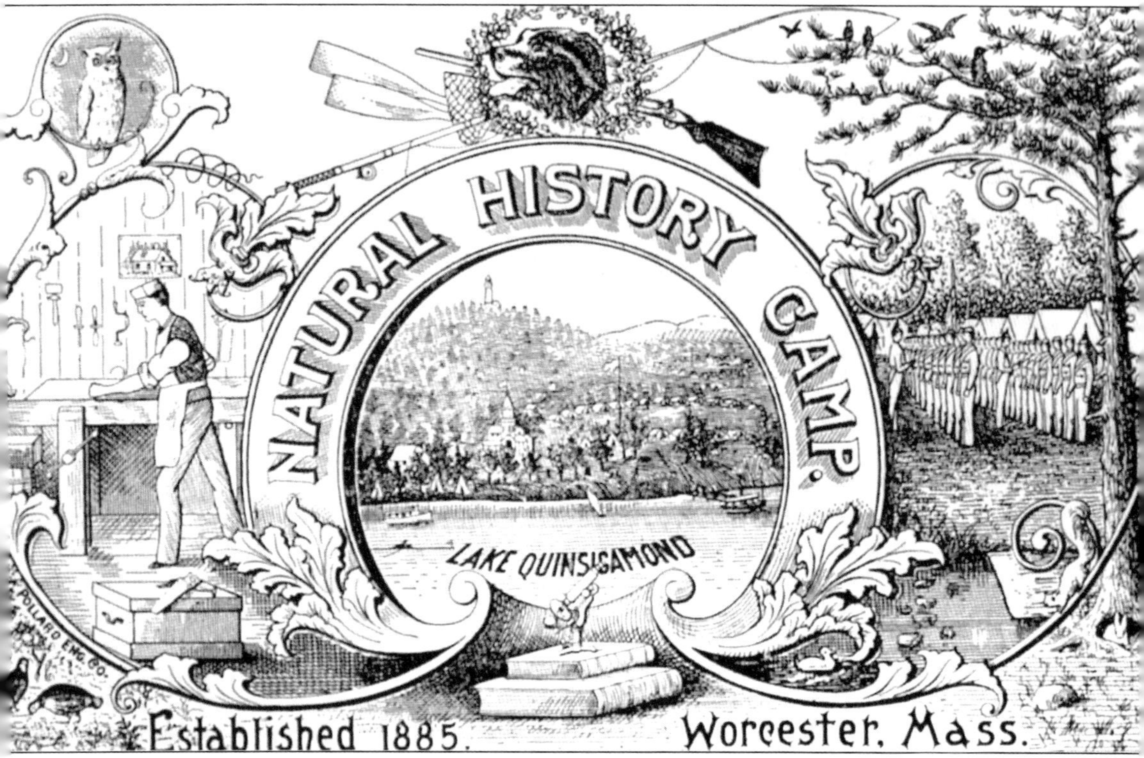

This woodcut advertising the Natural History Camp appeared in an 1890 booklet, which in turn was used to promote an extension of the Worcester and Shrewsbury Railroad through Shrewsbury center. The Natural History Camp allowed young men to learn more about nature. Dr. William Raymenton was in charge for many years, including one summer when he hatched a number of snake eggs borrowed from White City's Snake Den. The camp was located on what is now North Lake Avenue. A camp along similar lines, but exclusively for girls, stood on the opposite shore in Shrewsbury. The boys at Natural History Camp lived in tents and wore Civil War–style army uniforms. Several photos show the campers standing in military formation.

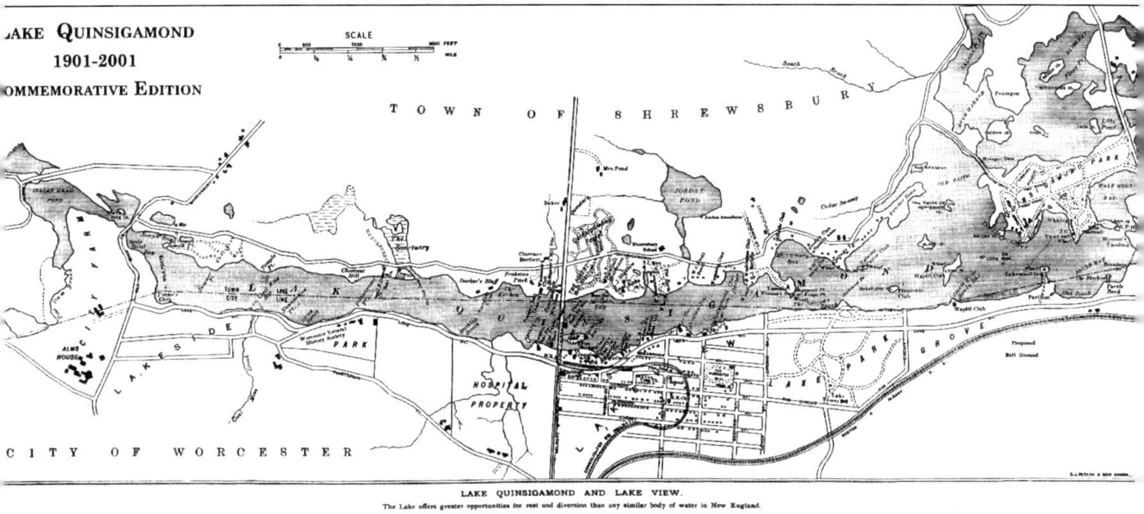

Lake Quinsigamond was in its heyday when this very detailed map of the lake and surrounding area was included as a foldout insert in the August 1901 edition of *Worcester Magazine*. This particular issue contained a lengthy article describing the many pleasures to be found at the lake, perhaps in an effort to entice more tourists to the area. The map incorporated many of the place names that had been chosen by a committee formed for that purpose in the late 1800s. A number of the selected place names were derived from the names of families living in the area, or were based upon popular nicknames for certain spots.

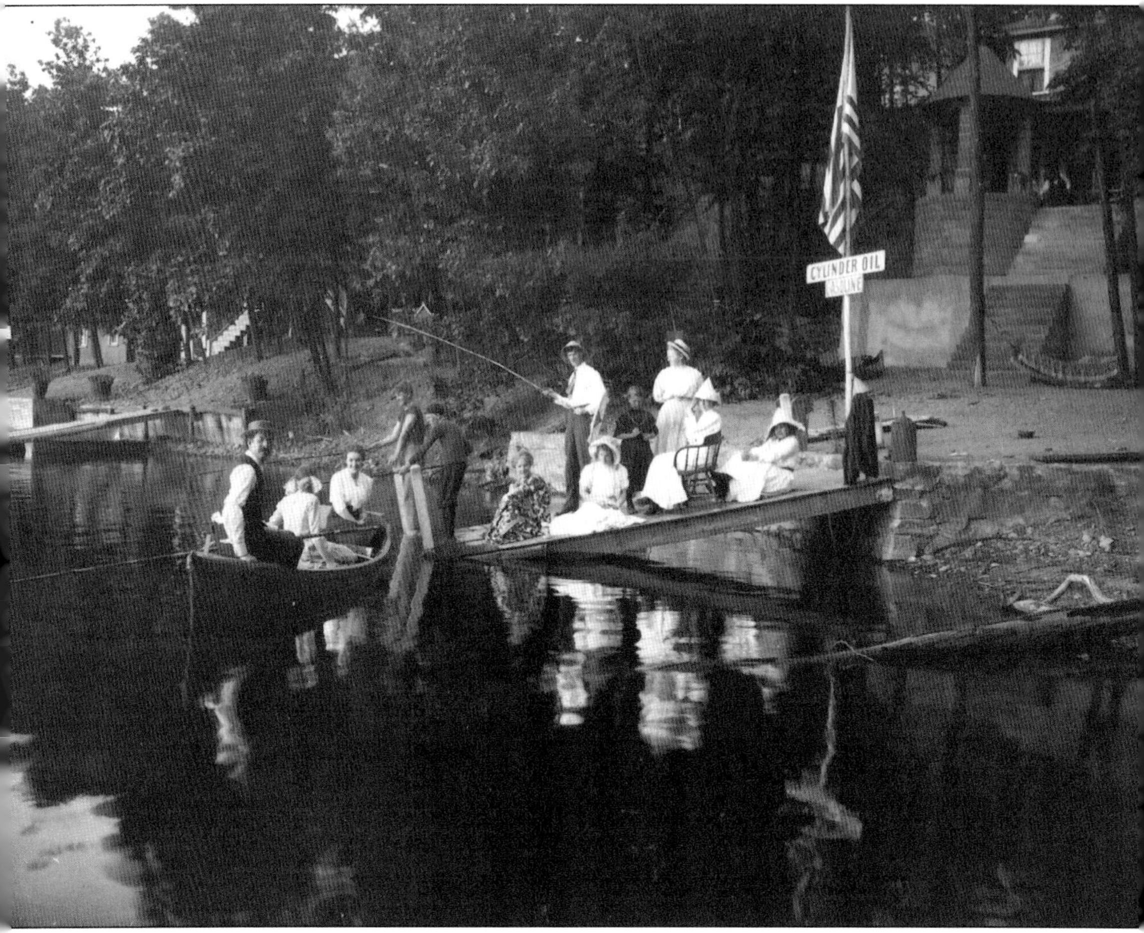

This photograph shows a group of people enjoying a summer's day at the lake—fishing, canoeing, and relaxing. The ladies on the dock appear to be sporting homemade paper hats to keep the sun off their faces. This clubhouse is reported to be the Englebrekt Club, a Swedish organization, on Lake Avenue. The club itself ran into some problems during the era of Prohibition—it was raided for serving liquor on at least a couple of occasions. One former resident recalls running down Lake Avenue as a young boy, chasing a group of police cars. The chase ended at the Englebrekt Club, where the police conducted a raid. The Englebrekt Club was popular for years, until finally being sold to the Marine Corps League. The building burned down, and a new structure is now being constructed on the site.

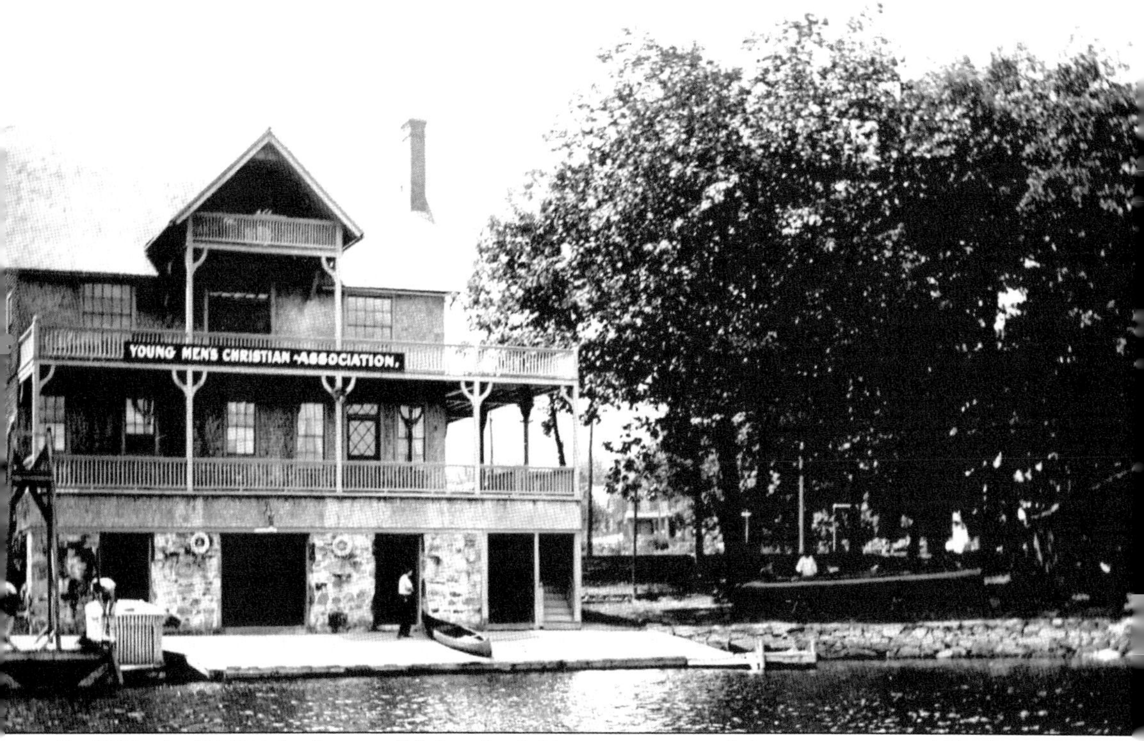

In 1889, the YMCA built a small lakeside clubhouse just east of the intersection of Sherbrook Avenue and Lake Avenue. In 1892, this clubhouse was replaced by the larger, more elaborate building shown here. The building measured 45 feet by 65 feet. Quarters were available for members to sleep at the club if they desired. Like many other organizations that had clubhouses at the lake, the YMCA maintained winter quarters in the city. A reception held at the club in 1892, typical of those held at many of the clubs, featured 200 Chinese lanterns for illumination, six fire balloons, and an orchestra. The steamer *Tatassit*, in addition to the many boats owned by the club, was secured to take the party guests on a tour of the lake. (Courtesy Barton Kamp.)

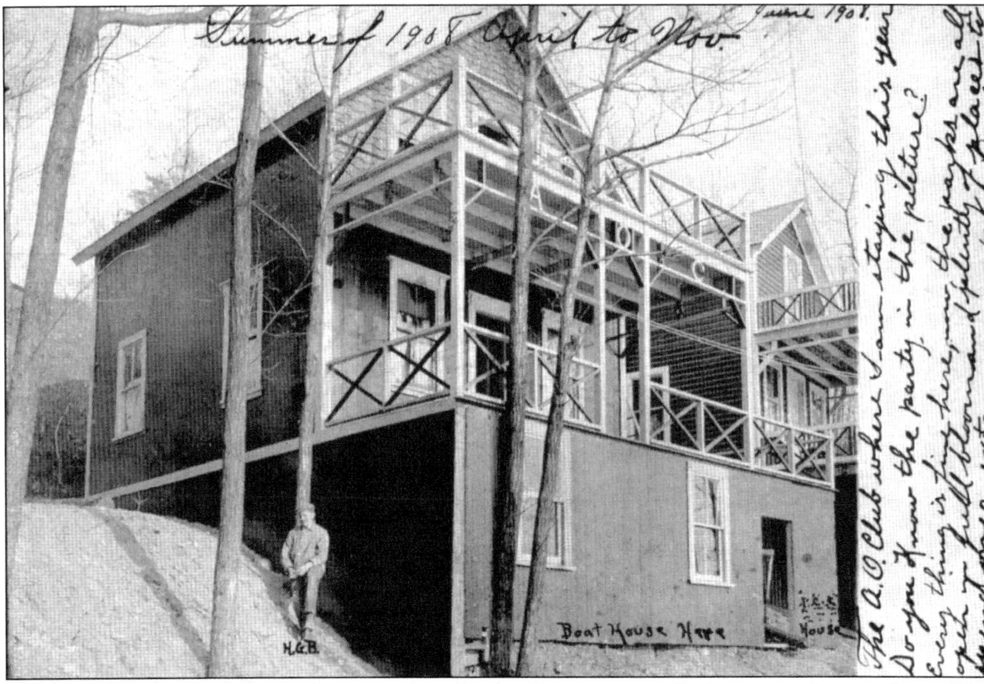

One of the many boathouses that once lined Lake Quinsigamond's shores can be seen here. The identity of this particular club is unknown. The building's construction is typical of many of the summer cottages and smaller clubs that once existed in the area. Most of the better-known boat clubs were larger, well-built structures, although it seems all were used only in the summer, with the exception of a few that were winterized in more modern times. (Courtesy Barton Kamp.)

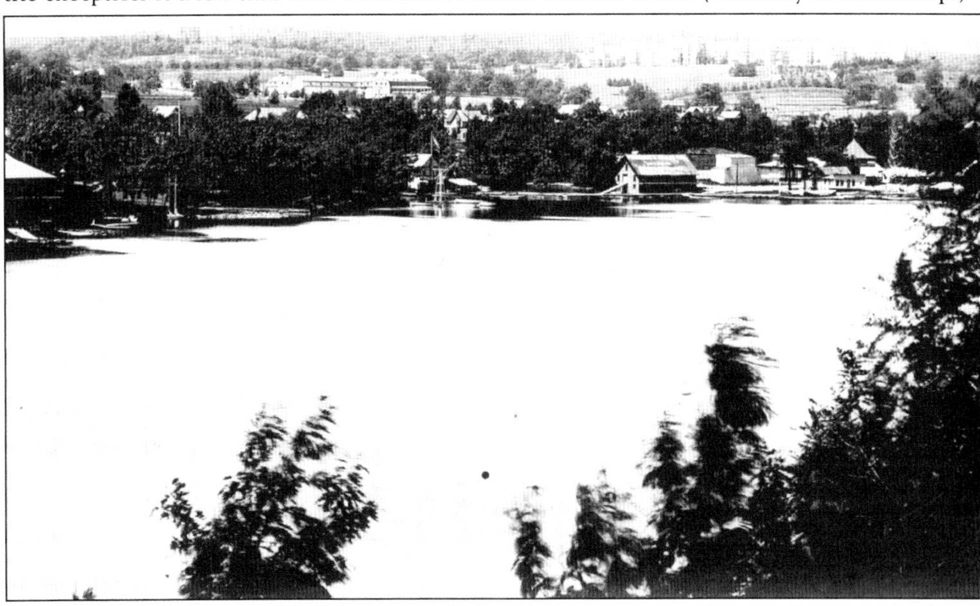

Judging from the obvious height from which this photograph was taken, it almost certainly was snapped from the top of the Eyrie Hotel. The hotel stood on a hill overlooking the lake. This view looks northwestward toward Lincoln Park. The Worcester Insane Asylum, as it was then known, can be seen on the top of the hill in the distance.

Four

Other Places and Attractions

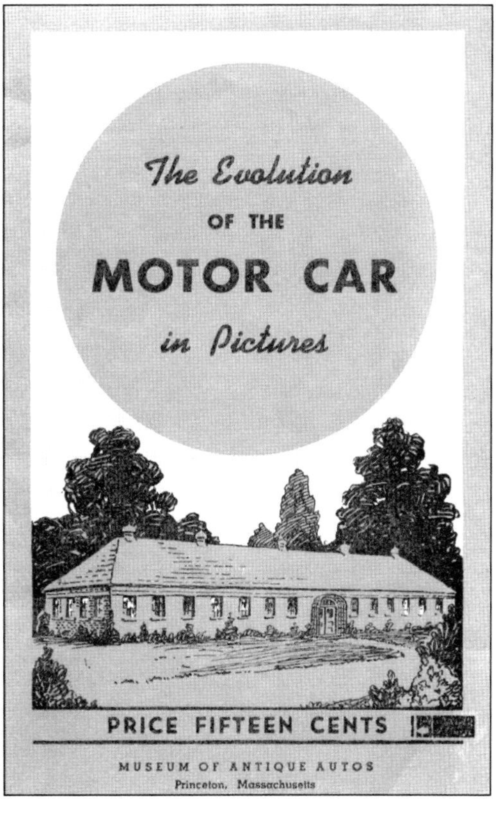

The Garganigo family operated the Museum of Antique Autos, which was housed in a brick building on Route 9, just east of the intersection with South Quinsigamond Avenue. The building still stands and houses a number of stores. The museum collection included many of the earliest automobiles. This brochure was illustrated with photographs of many vehicles in the museum's collection, and was used to advertise the museum shortly after it was moved to Princeton, Massachusetts, in the spring of 1938.

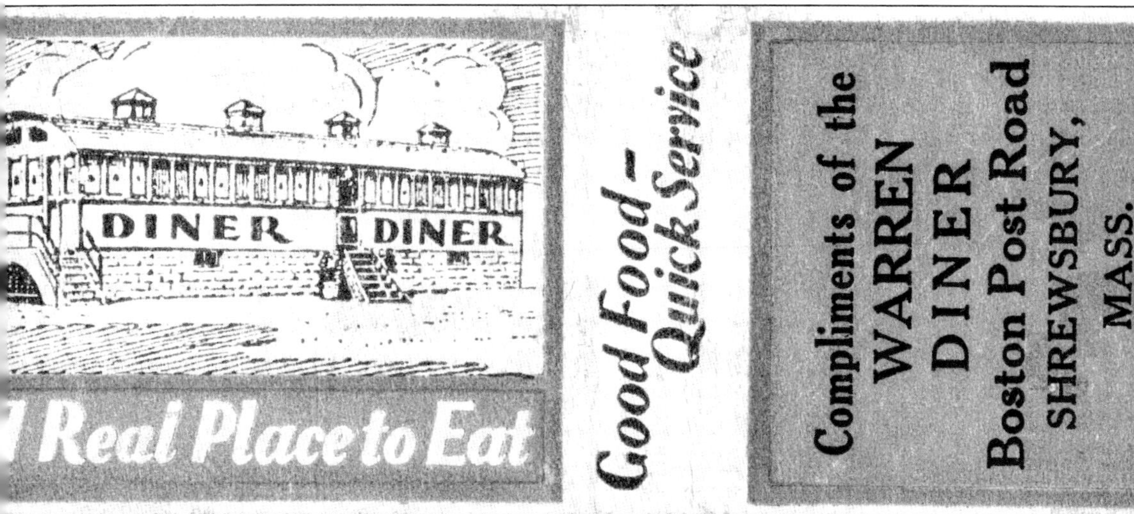

In 1926, the Crowe brothers, James and Joseph, opened a diner on the southeast corner of South Quinsigamond Avenue and Route 9. The diner, unlike almost all of its contemporaries, was built directly on site rather than in a factory. Crowe's Diner was quite large: 50 feet long and 14 feet wide. The eatery changed hands over the years, and was later known as Warren's Diner, Argento's Diner, then Wolf's Diner. For many years, it was open 24 hours a day. The diner no longer exists.

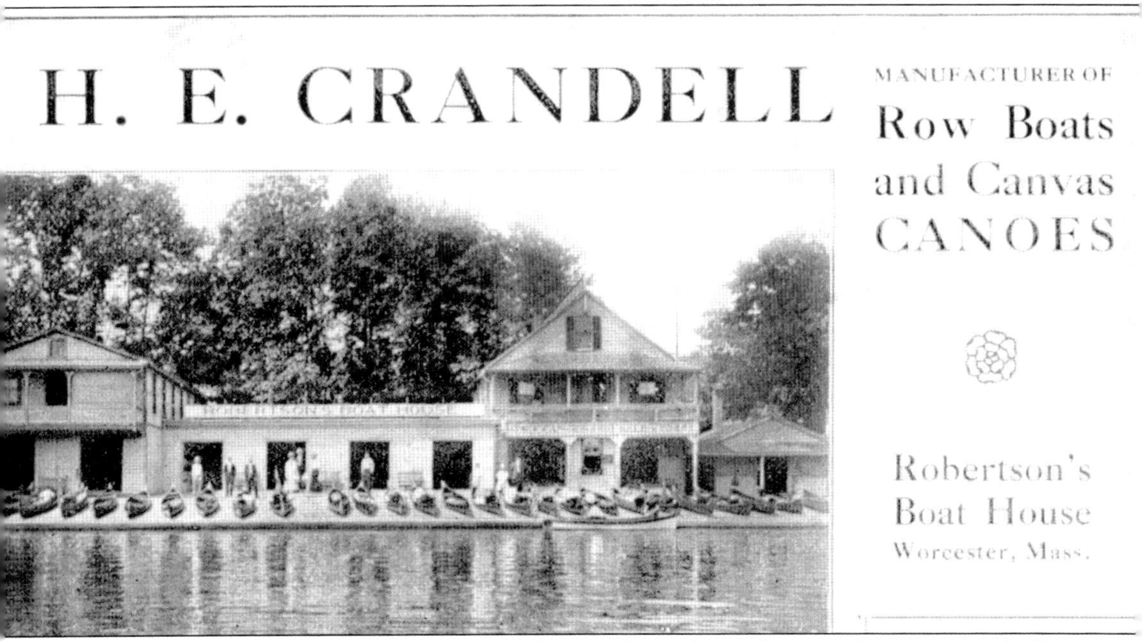

H. E. Crandell had a canoe-building business that was housed in Robertson's Boat House, which stood just south of Lincoln Park on Lake Avenue. For many years, Crandell's was well known for the quality of the canoes and rowboats built there. The most widely built types were the "Lake Quinsigamond model" canoe, which measured 17 feet long by 35 inches wide, and the "canvas-covered rowboat," which was produced in both 14-foot and 16-foot models. The canoe prices ranged from $40 to $55; rowboats cost $50 or $55. Eventually outboard motors were available for purchase, as well. In later years, Crandell's also served as a neighborhood gathering place. Many local residents still remember the good times spent at Crandell's. One couple who met there as young teenagers even wound up getting married! Pictured here is the cover from a brochure that was used to advertise Crandell's boats and canoes. (Courtesy John Richardson.)

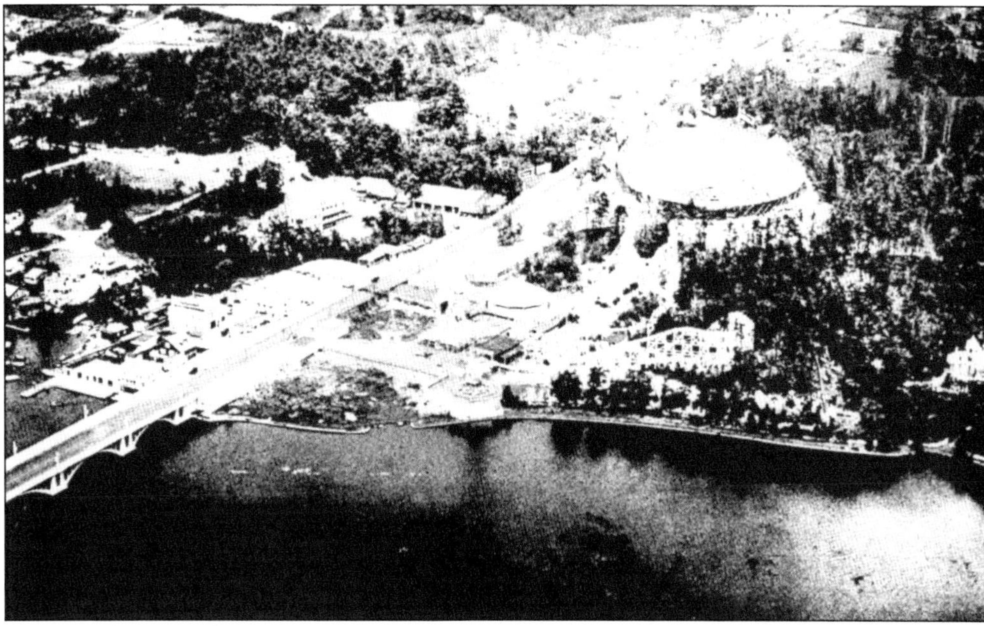

In the early 1920s, the Worcester County Coliseum was located in the area where White City East shopping center now stands. The coliseum was a track for bicycle and motorcycle racing. It is seen here, nestled between White City Amusement Park in the foreground and the Catholic Cemetery (later known as St. Anne's Cemetery), to the right of this scene. This photograph, an early aerial view, can be dated roughly between 1919 and 1923, as the new bridge (completed 1918–1919) is visible, but St. Anne's Church (completed 1923) is not yet built. After a few years, the track's popularity declined and the coliseum was razed.

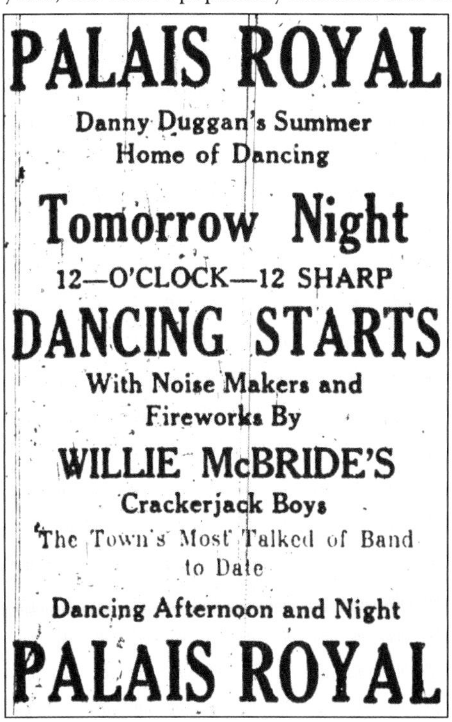

A summer dance hall, the Palais Royal stood at the northeast corner of Route 9 and North Quinsigamond Avenue. Originally, the business was to be named the Monte Carlo, but the proposed name was a bit too wild for the town fathers. The name was toned down a bit to the Palais Royal, which was just foreign enough to be exotic, but tame enough to satisfy the townspeople. The dance hall was a hot spot during the 1930s and 1940s, but its popularity later waned. Eventually, the business closed and the building was torn down.

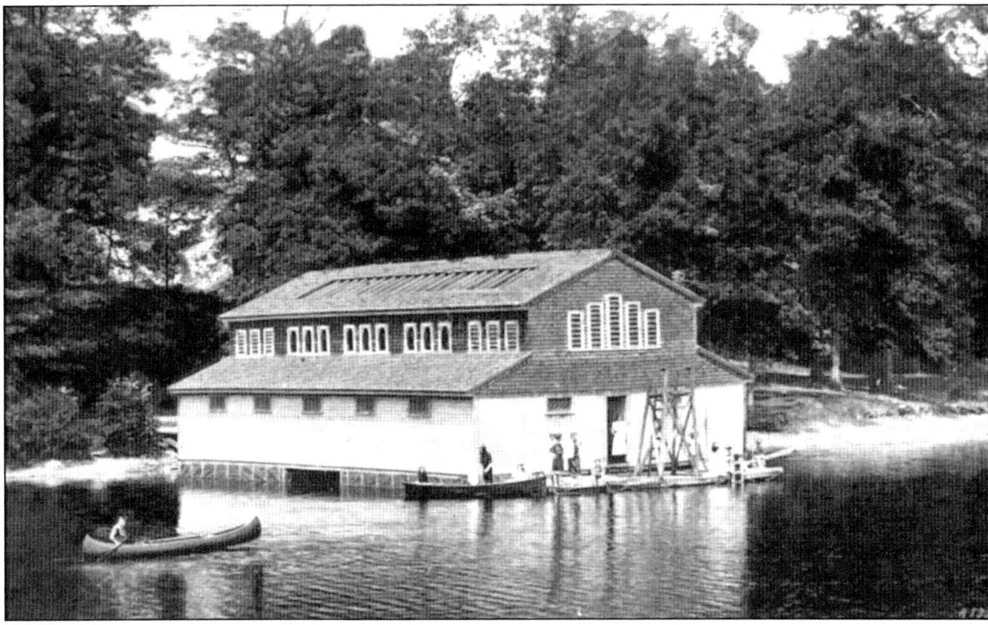

In the days before indoor plumbing became common, there were several bathhouses located on Lake Quinsigamond. The women's bathhouse shown here was located just to the north of the current Route 9 bridge. A few ladies can be seen standing on the dock in front of the building.

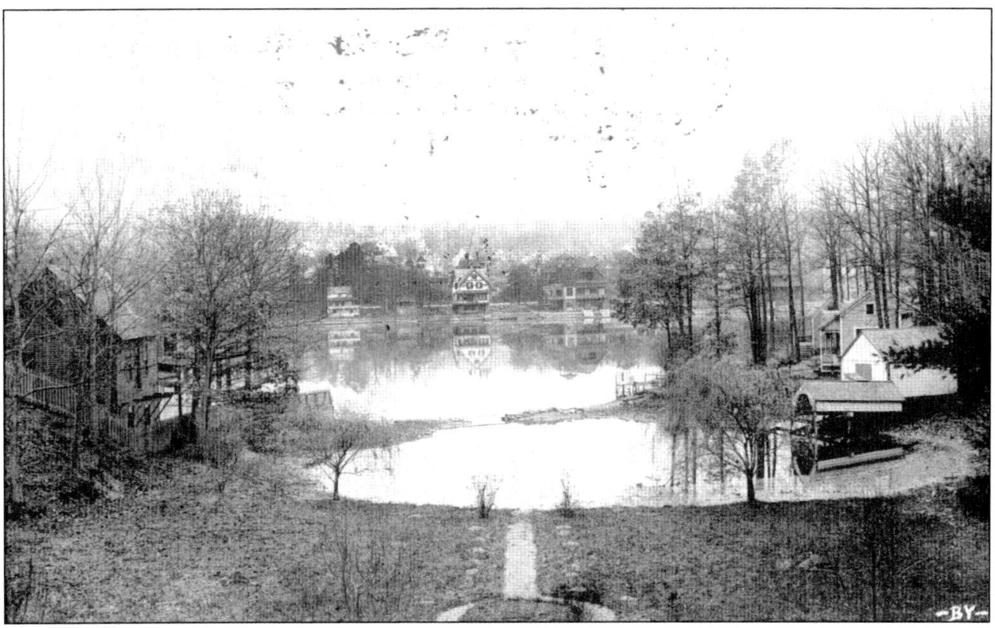

This postcard shows Horse Shoe Cove, which was located just south of the Bigelow Mansion on the Shrewsbury shore of Lake Quinsigamond. It was near here that Bigelow held an outing in October 1878 to honor none other that Benjamin Butler, the same man who had become well known as "Beast Butler" in Southern circles because of his harsh treatment of the citizens of New Orleans during the Civil War. Butler was running for political office in 1878. The outing was, according to the *Shrewsbury News*, a "lamentable failure," although it was fairly well attended. This area today has changed greatly in appearance due to the construction of several buildings.

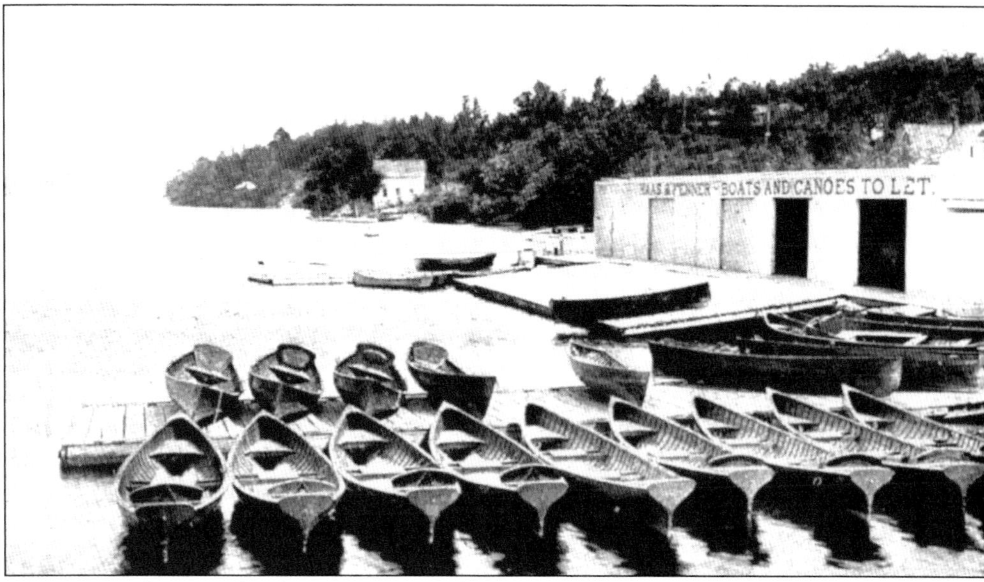

The Haas and Fenner boathouse was one of many that once called Lake Quinsigamond home. It was erected on the site of the Pond Tavern House, built to take advantage of the passenger traffic on the Boston and Worcester Turnpike, which opened in 1817. Situated right next to the present Route 9 bridge, the boathouse burned in the early 1960s.

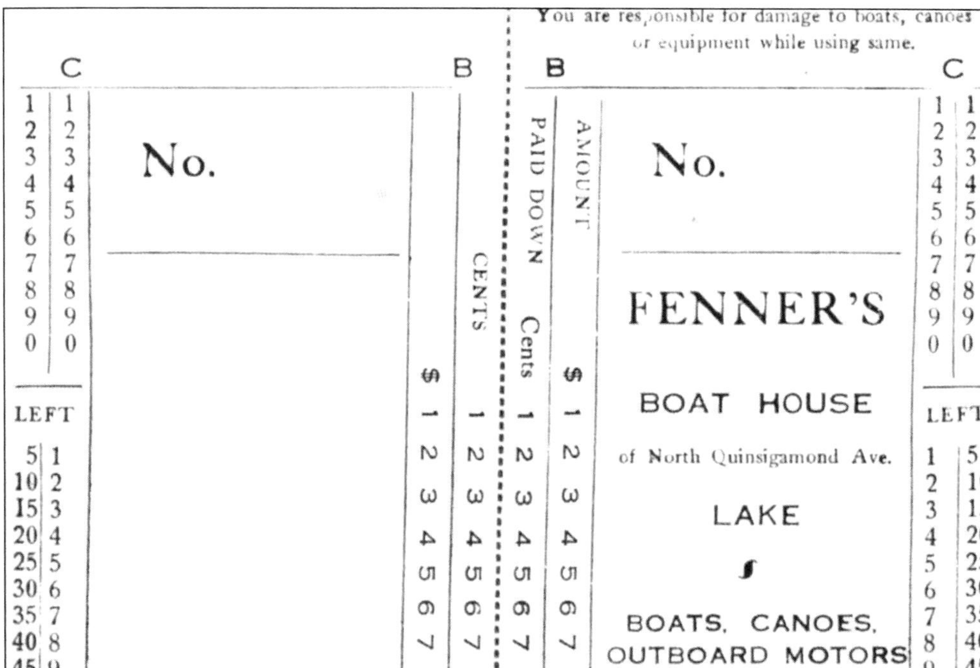

C B No. LEFT

You are responsible for damage to boats, canoes or equipment while using same.

B C PAID DOWN Cents AMOUNT $ CENTS

No.

FENNER'S

BOAT HOUSE

of North Quinsigamond Ave.

LAKE

BOATS, CANOES, OUTBOARD MOTORS

LEFT

The Haas and Fenner boathouse eventually became known as Fenner's. This ticket was used as both a bill and receipt—one half was kept at the business, the other was issued to the patron who rented a rowboat or canoe. The disclaimer states, "You are responsible for damage to boats, canoes, or equipment while using same." Eventually, thievery and vandalism of boats and canoes proved too costly, and all the boat rental businesses around the lake closed down.

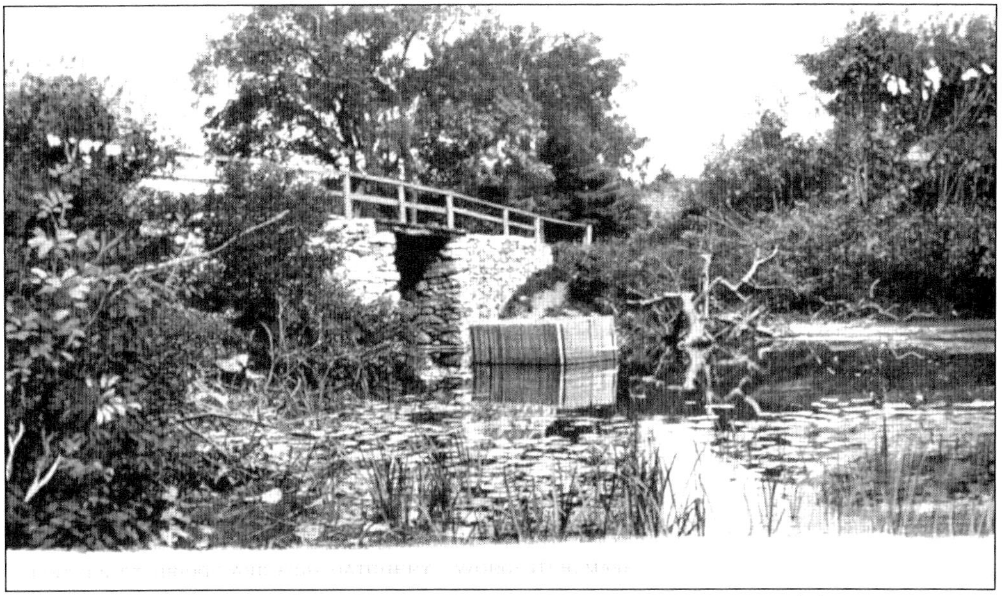

Lincoln Street spans Lake Quinsigamond at its northern end. It is reported that Gen. George Washington passed over this old crossing point on one of his visits through Shrewsbury. The bridge in this view is long gone, but a much more modern bridge stands at this very spot today.

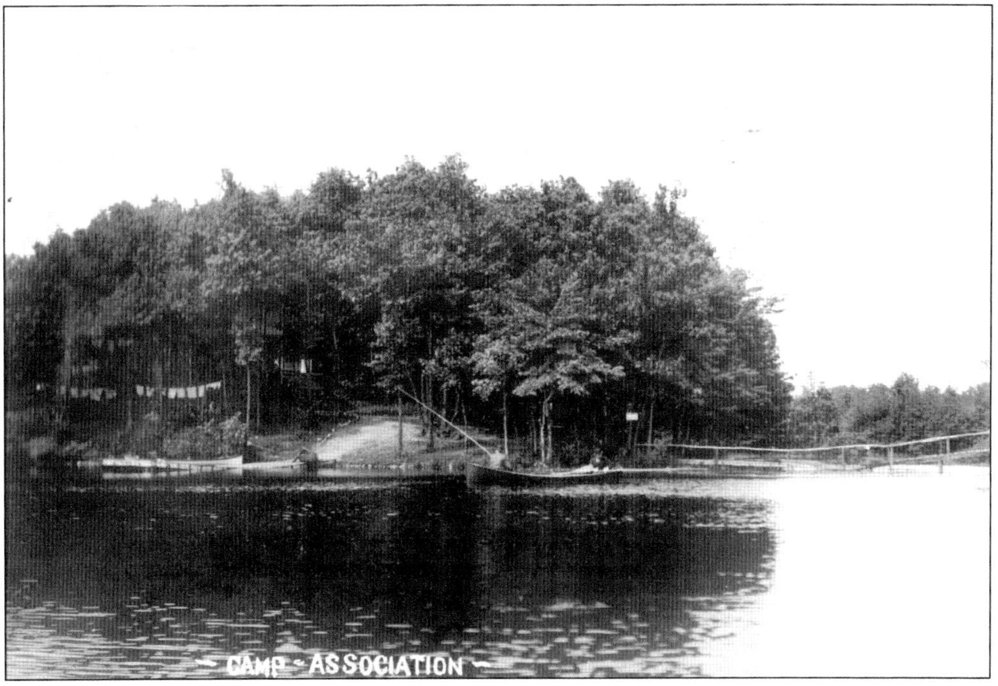

The camp association referred to on this postcard view refers to a group that used what was then known as Camp Island as a camping area in the summer. One can still see the island and take in this view from the point where the Lincoln Street Bridge crosses Lake Quinsigamond, looking northward. (Courtesy Barton Kamp.)

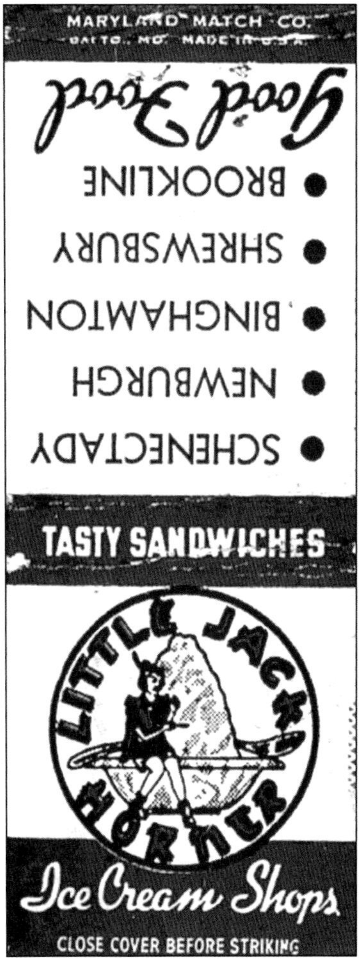

The Little Jack Horner Ice Cream Shop was in operation during the 1940s. It was one of many businesses established to take advantage of the huge crowds that frequented the area around White City Park during that time. The shop stood in the area currently known as White City East. It was only open for a few years. Another business later stood roughly in the same location: Harry's was a hugely popular spot, especially with the late-night crowd. The menu at Harry's was printed on old metal Venetian blinds.

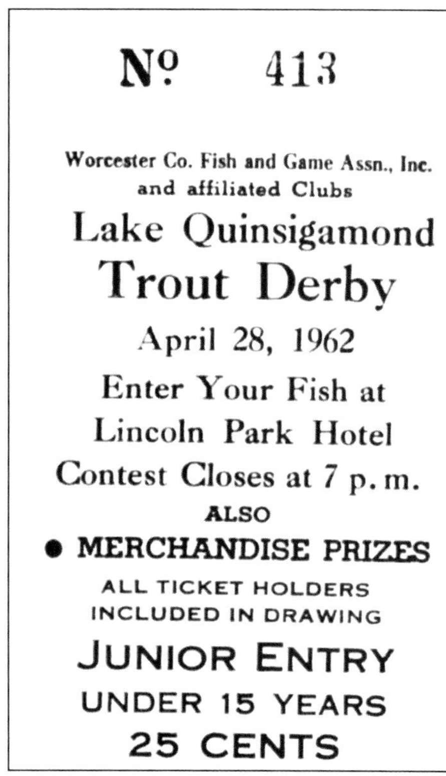
№ 413

Worcester Co. Fish and Game Assn., Inc.
and affiliated Clubs

Lake Quinsigamond
Trout Derby

April 28, 1962

Enter Your Fish at
Lincoln Park Hotel
Contest Closes at 7 p.m.

ALSO

• MERCHANDISE PRIZES

ALL TICKET HOLDERS
INCLUDED IN DRAWING

JUNIOR ENTRY
UNDER 15 YEARS
25 CENTS

Lake Quinsigamond has long been known as an excellent place to go fishing, and it has been the site of many fishing derbies over the years, often on the opening day of fishing season. Two popular examples were the Coolidge School Sunrise Trout Derby and the Lake Quinsigamond Trout Derby, headquartered at the old Lincoln Park Hotel. This ticket, recently discovered in a dresser drawer, belonged to the first-place winner in the junior division of the 1962 contest—by coincidence, the author of this book.

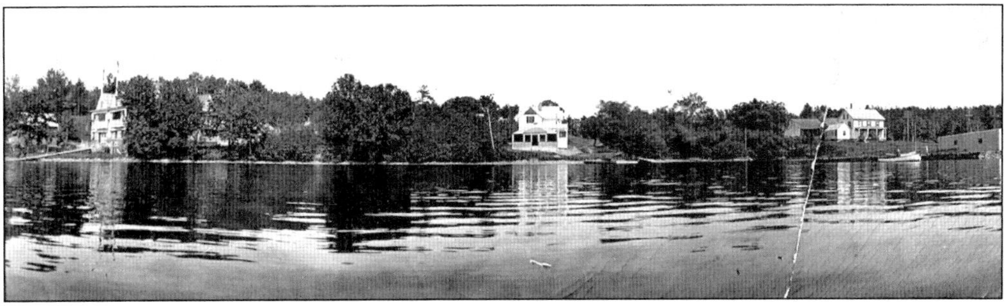

This is an early panoramic photograph showing the Shrewsbury shore across from what is now Regatta Point. The building on the far right in this scene is the Haas and Fenner boathouse. Unlike the southern end of the lake, the area north of the causeway or Route 9 bridge did not contain many clubhouses or other buildings. The Frohsinn Club, located on the left in this view, was one exception, and was one of the earliest clubhouses built on Lake Quinsigamond. Today, this same area is almost completely lined with buildings. (Courtesy Michael Paika.)

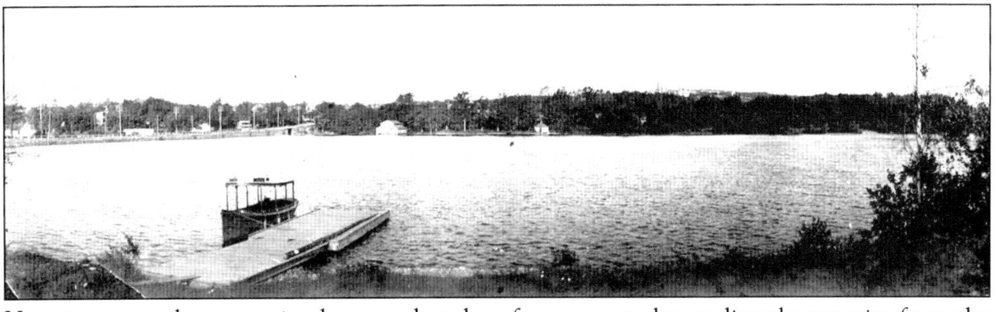

Here is a second panoramic photograph, taken from a spot almost directly opposite from the previous view. This view looks westward toward the Worcester shore and what today is the Regatta Point State Park. The recently constructed boathouse at Regatta Point would be almost directly in the middle of this view today. The boat at the dock may be one of the many steam launches—smaller versions of the large passenger-carrying steamboats—that were popular in the days before outboard motors came on the scene. (Courtesy Michael Paika.)

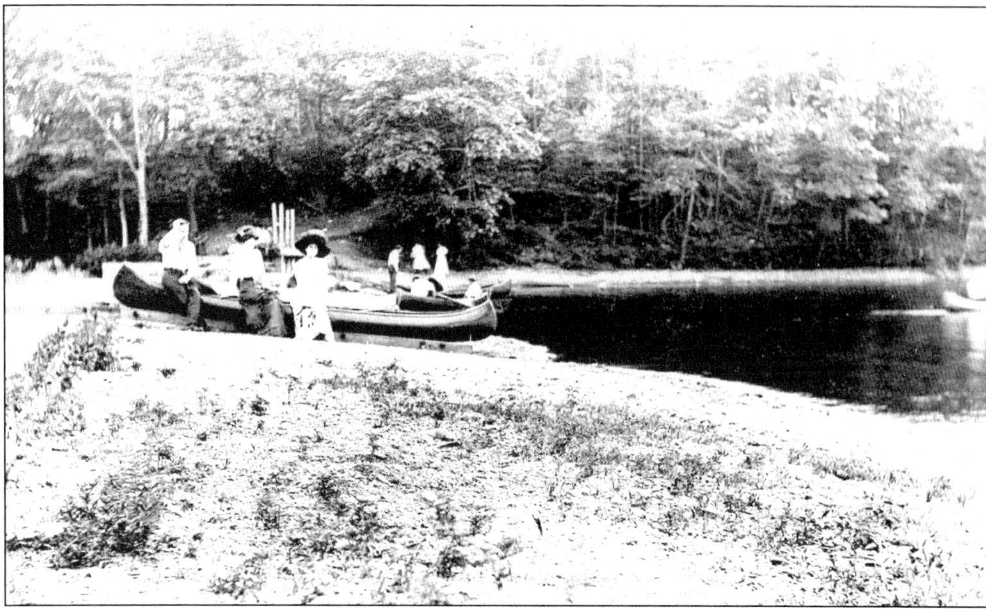

This photograph shows a group of people out for a canoe ride, stopped for a rest or perhaps a picnic. The specific location of this photograph is not identified, but it is at Lake Quinsigamond in the summer of 1910. The location looks very much like the Stringer Dam area at Sunset Beach, with the hill in the background leading up to the Edgemere Boulevard area.

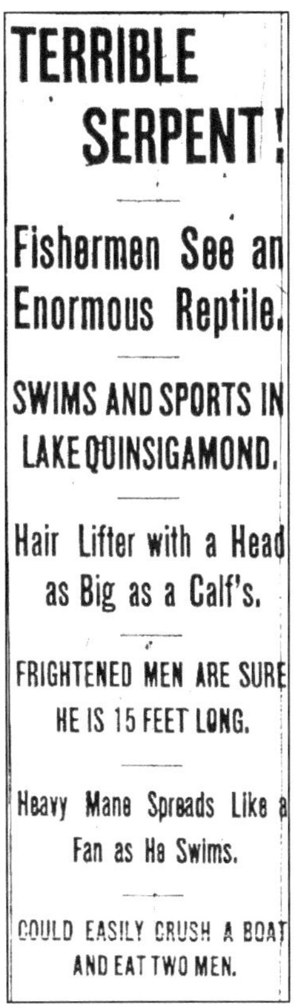

TERRIBLE SERPENT!

Fishermen See an Enormous Reptile.

SWIMS AND SPORTS IN LAKE QUINSIGAMOND.

Hair Lifter with a Head as Big as a Calf's.

FRIGHTENED MEN ARE SURE HE IS 15 FEET LONG.

Heavy Mane Spreads Like a Fan as He Swims.

COULD EASILY CRUSH A BOAT AND EAT TWO MEN.

In 1896, two Worcester men, out for a fishing trip on Flint Pond, were scared half to death by what they were sure was a sea serpent. A panic quickly ensued as the story spread. People were afraid to swim in the lake, men went serpent hunting with shotguns, and little old ladies wouldn't venture out for boat rides. A psychic known as the White Mahatma was consulted, but the seer only said the creature either "does not exist, or exists only in someone's mind." The uproar eventually subsided, with one observation that may help to explain the story: several newspaper accounts mentioned that neither of the men who saw the serpent had "drank a drop of liquor in over 12 years."

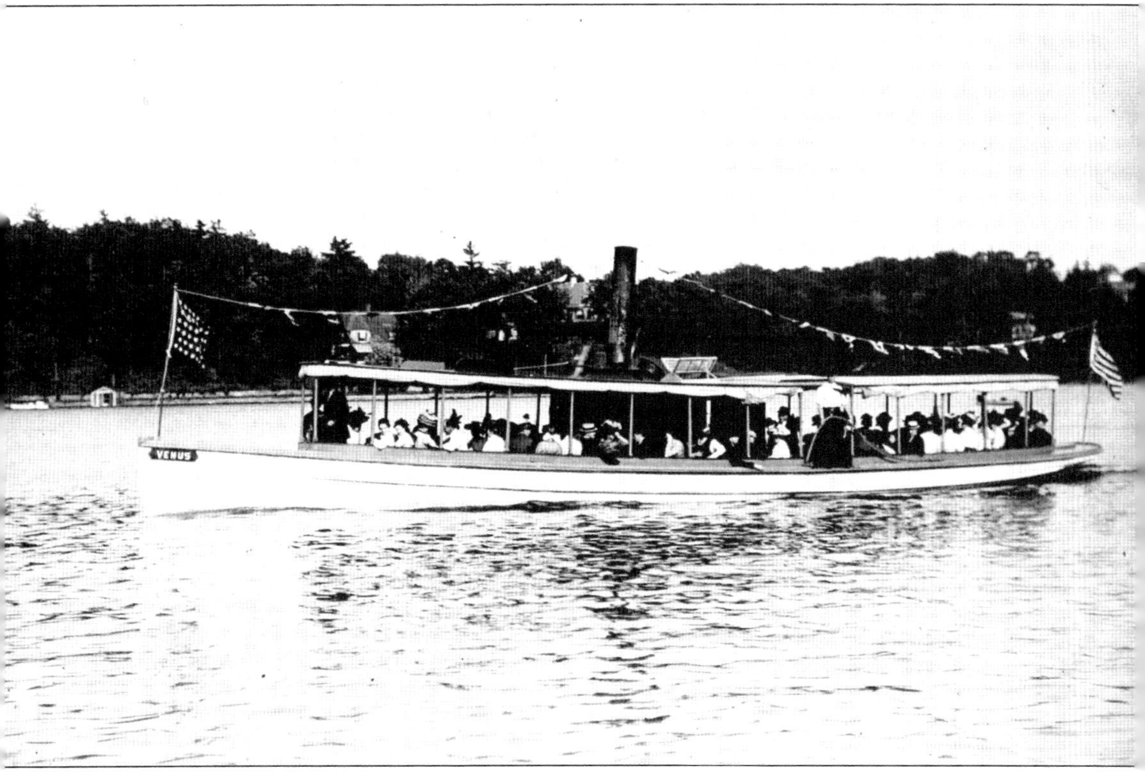

The *Venus* was one of the larger steamboats to ply the waters of Lake Quinsigamond in the late 1800s. Competition for passengers between the various steamboat owners was constant. In at least one case this resulted in a dispute over which boats were licensed to stop at the various docks maintained by clubs and hotels on the Shrewsbury shore, thereby effectively cutting out half of that particular owner's business until the matter was resolved. Eventually, there were far more passengers than the boats could hold, resulting in long waits for a boat ride. On one occasion, overcrowding resulted in the disastrous collapse of the upper deck of the steamer *Colonel Isaac Davis*. Five people were killed and many more injured in this accident. (Courtesy Barton Kamp.)

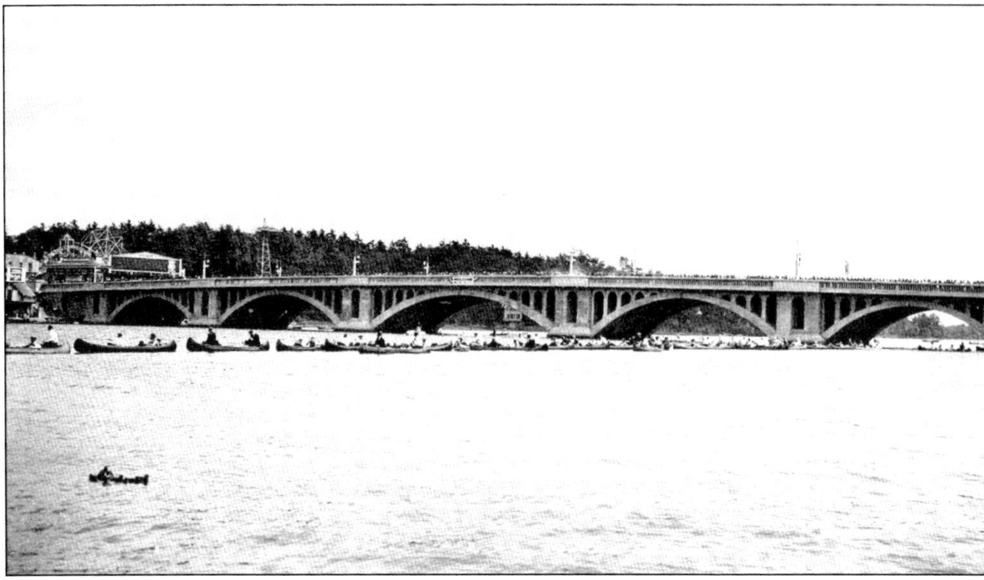

Even after the introduction of motorboats, canoes were still very popular at Lake Quinsigamond. Many canoes are visible in this photograph, possibly lined up for a boat parade or to watch a crew race. This particular photograph was used for a colored postcard view.

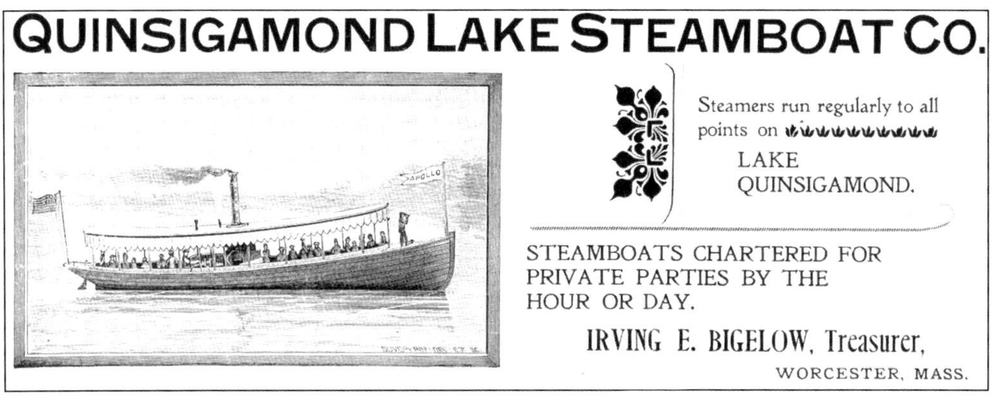

The *Apollo* was in service during the 1880s and 1890s, and was taken out of service in 1903. The boat's owner, Irving Bigelow, was the son of the creator of White City Park, H. H. Bigelow. When the park opened in 1905, the boat was sold to someone who was planning to place it in the park. While finishing the boardwalk area, workers found that the old boat was in the way. The workmen approached the elder Bigelow for permission to dismantle the old craft. Not knowing of the sale of the steamboat or the new owner's plans, H. H. Bigelow gave his authorization to have the boat destroyed. Upon learning of the boat's demise, the new owner flew into a rage, but it was too late to bring the steamboat back to life.

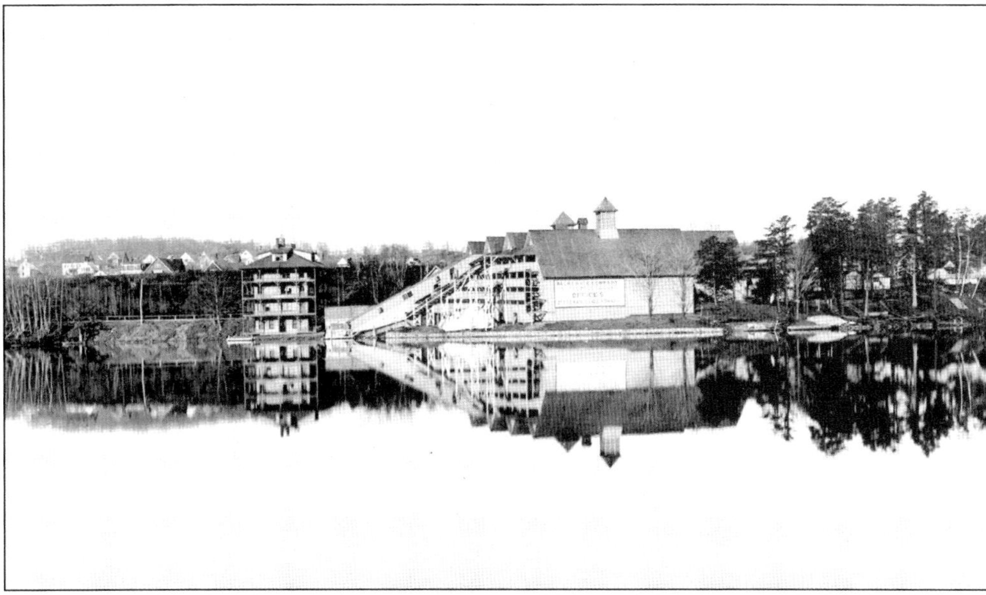

During the winter months, there was much less activity around Lake Quinsigamond. But of course, there were skating parties, ice fishing, and the occasional iceboat. The iceboats proved to be dangerous and were eventually banned from the lake altogether. Ice harvesting was another winter activity on the lake. The Walker Ice Company had icehouses on the Worcester shore, where the ice would be brought for storage, to be sold during the summer months. (Courtesy Erik Larson.)

This stereopticon card photograph was taken *c.* 1865 at Lake Quinsigamond, in the days when it was still known as Long Pond. This card was one of a series of views, most of which contained what, at the time, would have been more interesting subjects than this scene of a man sitting on a fence. This particular image is significant to us today, however. The view looks southward from the causeway, and shows just how undeveloped the shores of the lake were at the time. (Courtesy Erik Larson.)

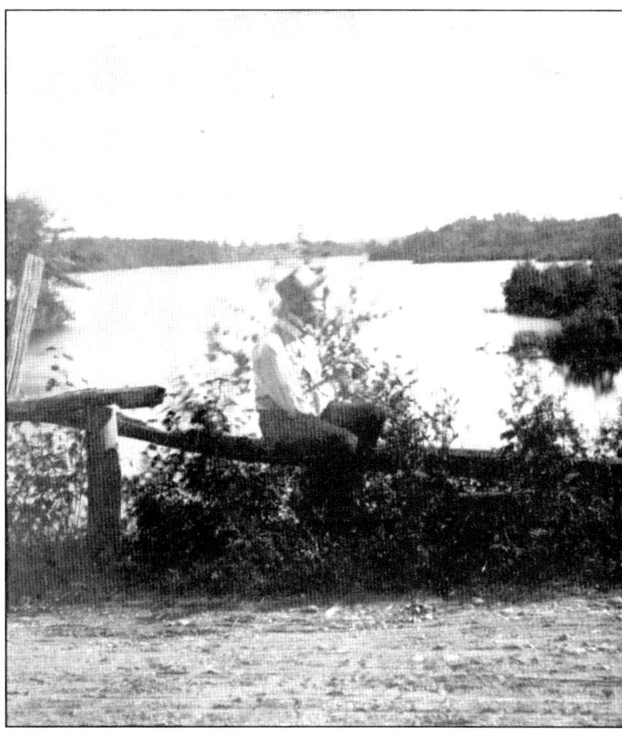

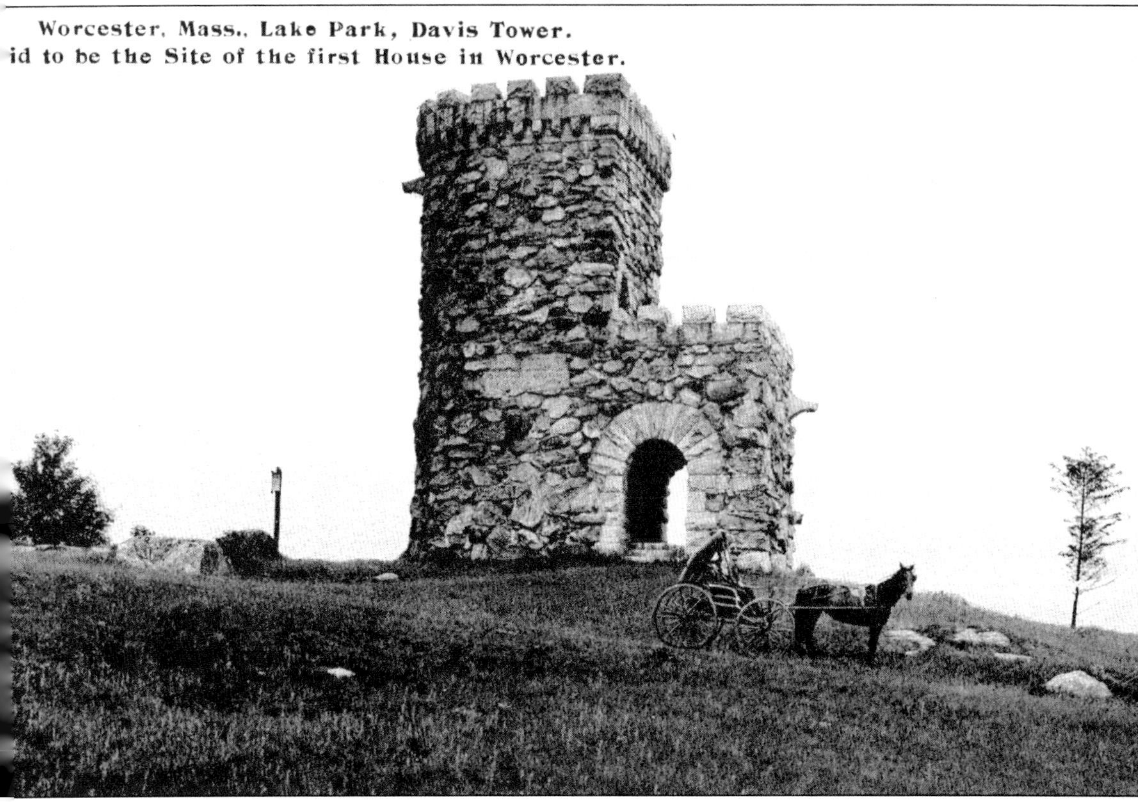

The Davis Tower was erected at the corner of what is now Hamilton Street and Coburn Avenue, in Quinsigamond State Park. It was named after, and built by, Isaac Davis, a man who played a prominent role in developing the lake area. He also donated much of the land in the area where the tower stood. The tower was used as an observation point to obtain views of Lake Quinsigamond, and several images photographed from the tower were made into postcards. This location was also the site of the first house built in Worcester, from where the owner's son was carried off by Native Americans. The boy was later reunited with his family when two female captives killed their kidnappers and returned the boy to his home. Recently, the tower was torn down after it was deemed unsafe.

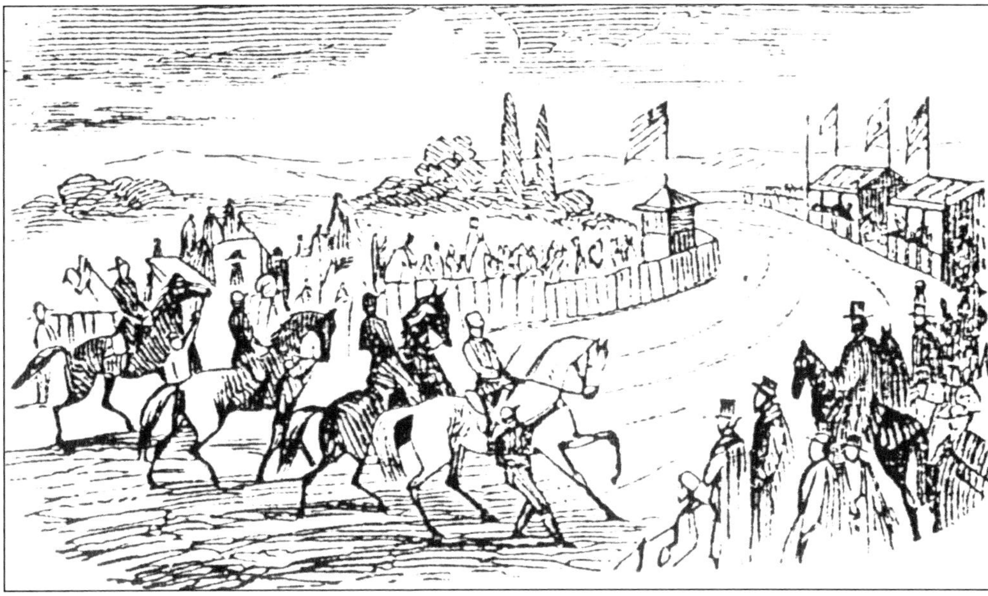

Few people living in the Edgemere section of Shrewsbury realize that the streets they travel on were once part of a horse-racing track. The Full Moon Driving (or Trotting) Park was a popular attraction in the 1870s. This track had been built many years earlier, fallen into disuse, and then was reopened in 1877. Complete with stables, the track was a mile long. Many spectators would spend the day at the track and nearby Quinsigamond Park. The track itself was oval shaped, following the outlines of what today are Edgemere Boulevard and Lakeside Drive.

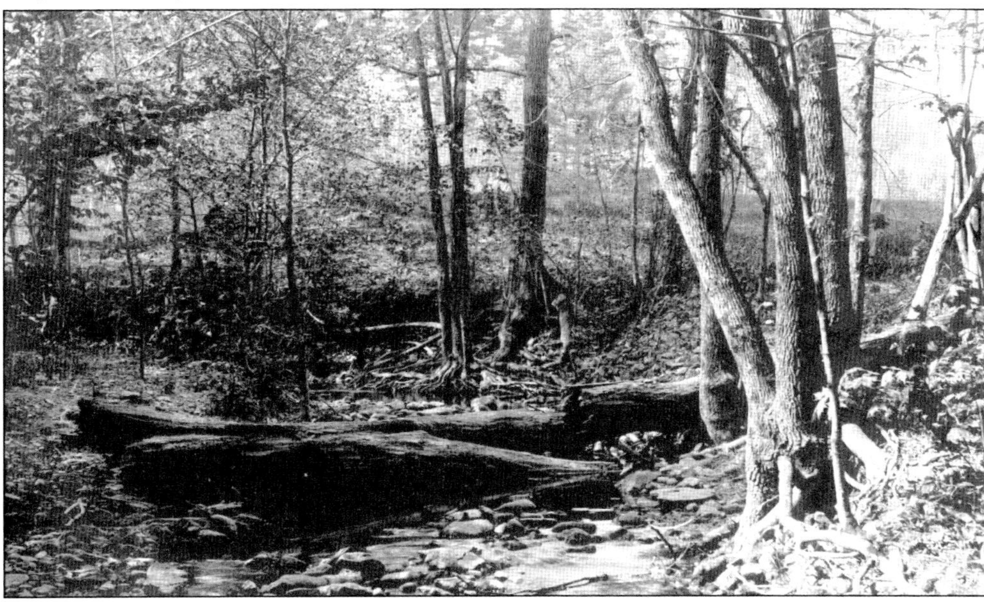

Coal Mine Brook runs into Lake Quinsigamond north of Wigwam Hill. Many people wonder where the brook got its name. Early settlers found anthracite coal near here, which was used to make paint. Later, a coal mine was dug to a depth of 300 feet, and small cars and a windlass were used to bring the coal to the surface. The coal was found to be of poor quality, and the whole operation was shut down, but not before the little brook that ran nearby had been named after the coal mine.

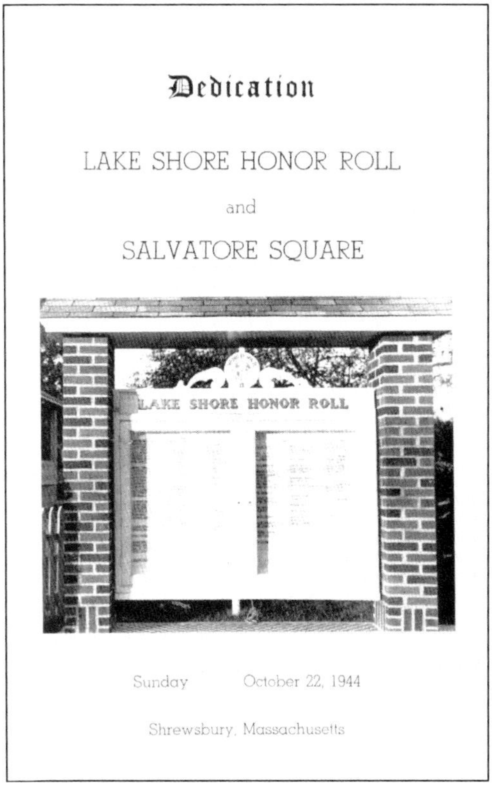

Dedication

LAKE SHORE HONOR ROLL

and

SALVATORE SQUARE

LAKE SHORE HONOR ROLL

Sunday October 22, 1944

Shrewsbury, Massachusetts

During World War II, people from the lake neighborhood decided to erect an honor roll to recognize those local residents who were serving in the armed forces. The Lake Shore Honor Roll was located at the corner of John Street and South Quinsigamond Avenue. The location was named after Private Harold Salvatore, an 18-year-old Lake Shore resident who had been killed while serving in the Marines. The honor roll was dedicated on October 22, 1944. It stood for many years until a portion was removed and replaced by a bench. The structure was later torn down.

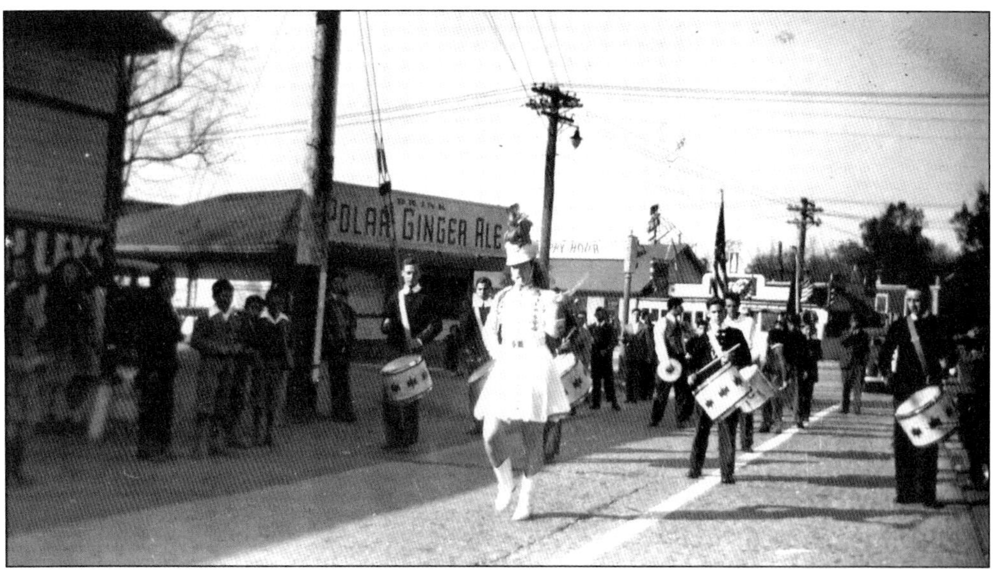

As part of the dedication ceremonies for the Lake Shore Honor Roll, a parade was held. The parade began at Route 9 and followed South Quinsigamond Avenue to the corner where the honor roll was located. The Veterans of Foreign Wars Drum Corps was featured in the parade, and is seen here passing by part of White City Amusement Park.

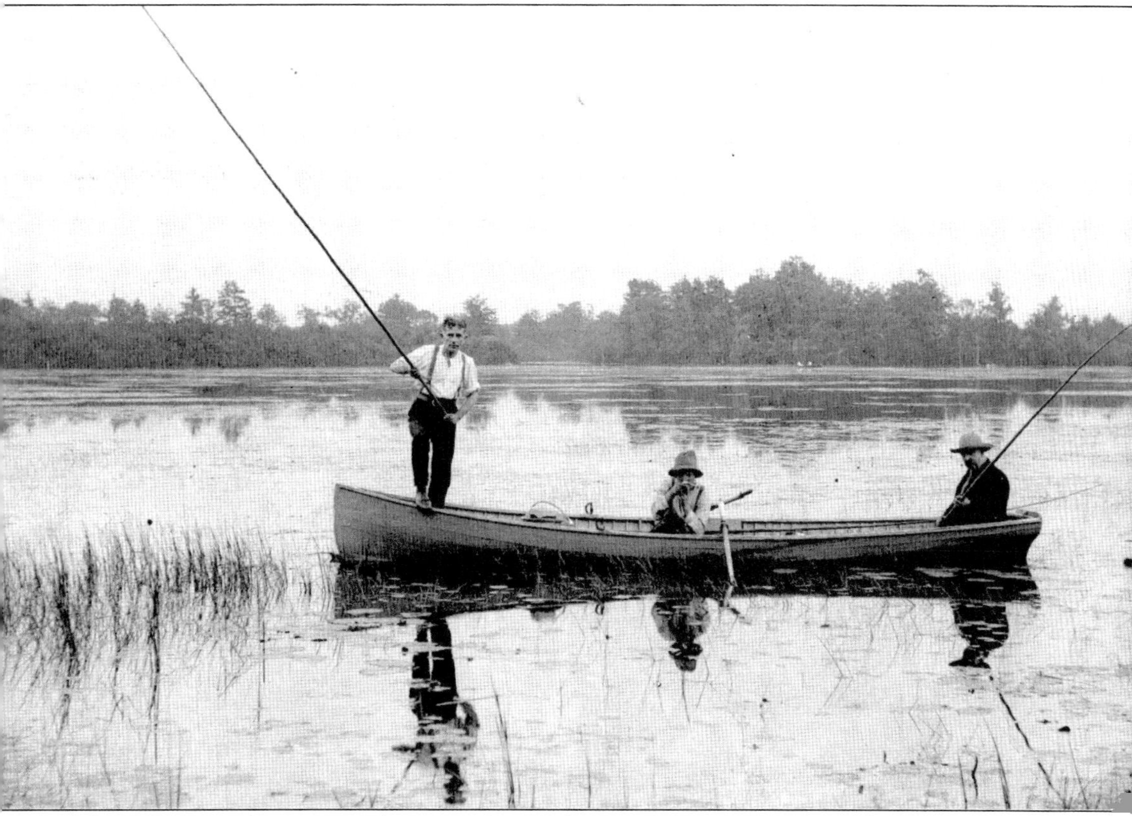

Fishing has long been a popular pastime at Lake Quinsigamond. In fact, the lake's name is derived from the Native American word for "long-nosed fishing place," or a place to fish for pickerel. Some old accounts tell of anglers returning home with what would today be considered amazing amounts of fish. On many occasions over the years, fishing derbies were held at Lake Quinsigamond, mostly on opening day of fishing season. Hundreds, perhaps thousands, of fishermen would line the shores starting before dawn. Three old-time anglers are shown here, enjoying a relaxing day of fishing on the lake. (Courtesy Barton Kamp.)

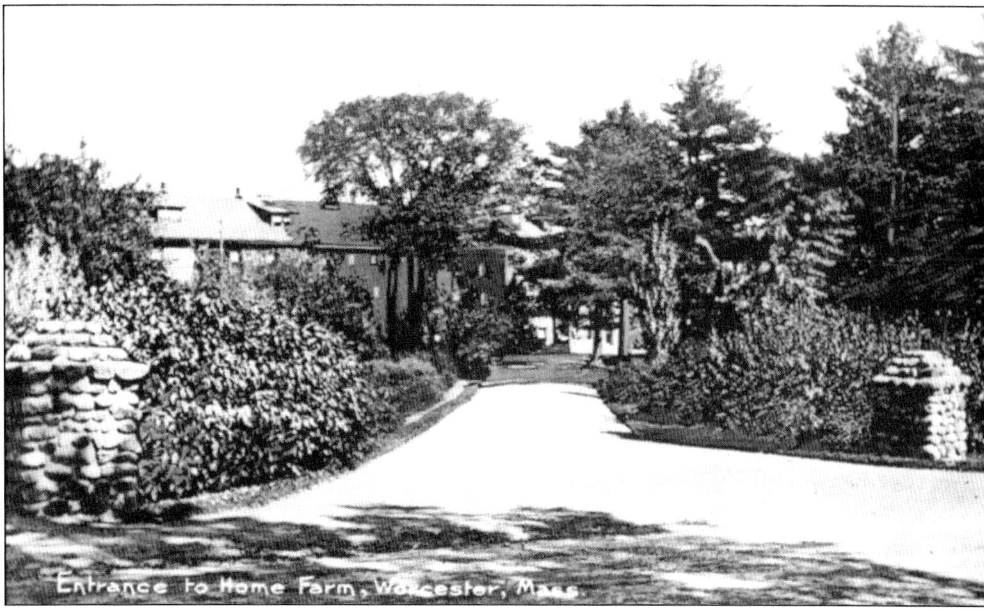

The Home Farm, or Poor Farm, stood at the northern end of Lake Quinsigamond. For many years, this is where Worcester's poorest residents lived. Although occupancy had dwindled considerably by the 1950s, the farm was still in use when the terrible tornado of 1953 roared straight through the grounds, killing a number of people living there. The Home Farm ceased operations within a short time after the disaster.

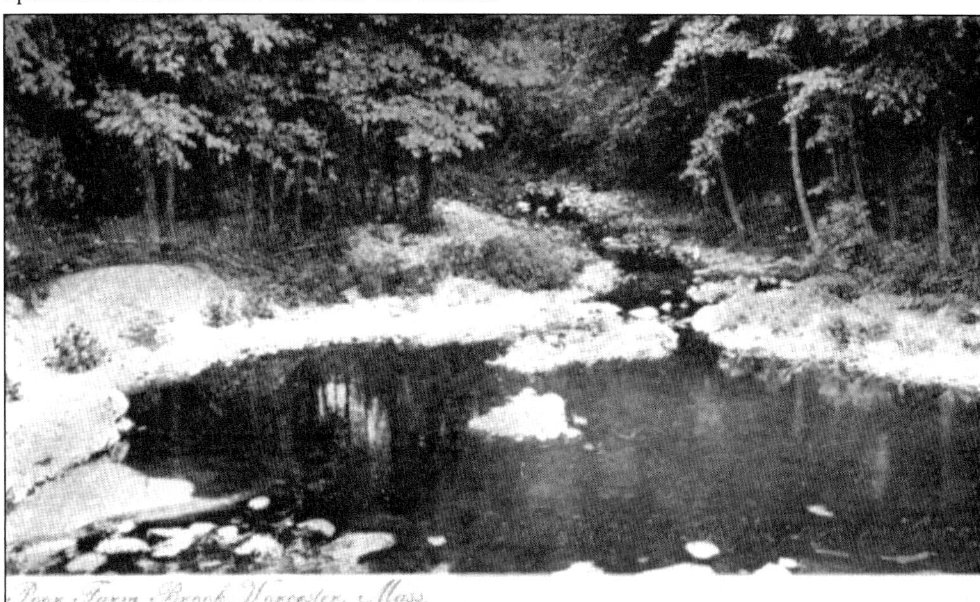

Poor Farm Brook ran through Worcester's Home Farm, right into the northern end of Lake Quinsigamond. In the times before modern trash disposal, the city of Worcester hauled its garbage to the farm and fed it to a large herd of pigs. Unfortunately the pigs used the brook to wallow in, thus polluting the brook and a good portion of the lake. After many complaints, Shrewsbury's selectmen took action to have the pigs removed. The city finally evicted the pigs after a long battle, and soon the north end of the lake was again suitable for swimming.

Bronzo's was a nightclub and restaurant that stood at the corner of Route 9 and North Quinsigamond Avenue. It was well known for its floorshows, and was a popular function facility. The business operated until the 1960s, when the building was torn down and replaced by a fast-food restaurant. One of the many acts that appeared at Bronzo's was the famous comedian Jackie Mason.

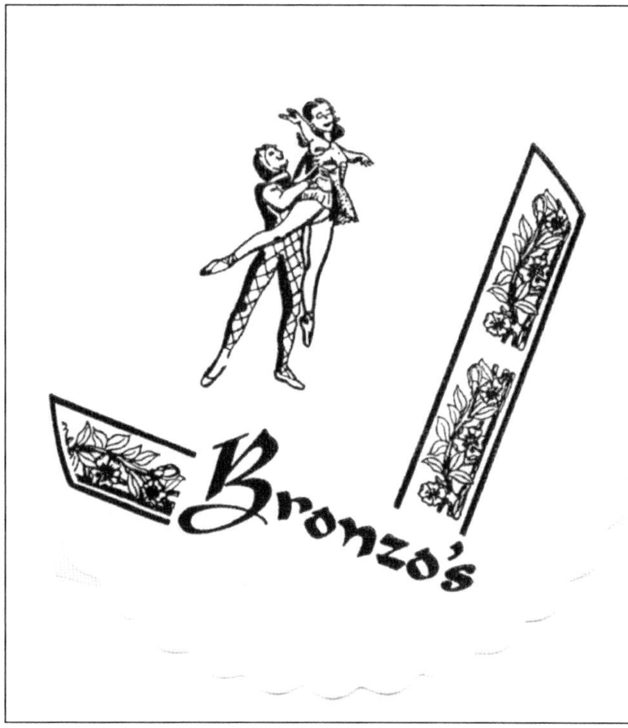

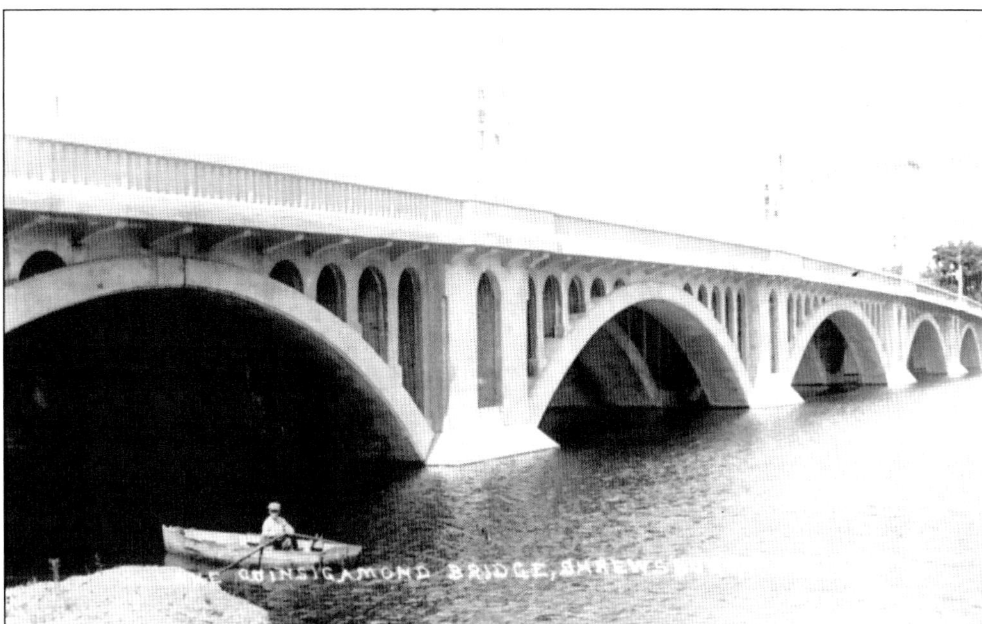

The Lake Quinsigamond Bridge was dedicated in July 1919 with a huge ceremony. It replaced the earlier dirt causeway. Even though it has been modernized, the bridge mostly retains its original look. The young boy in the rowboat probably rented the vessel from the Haas and Fenner boathouse, which would be just out of view to the right.

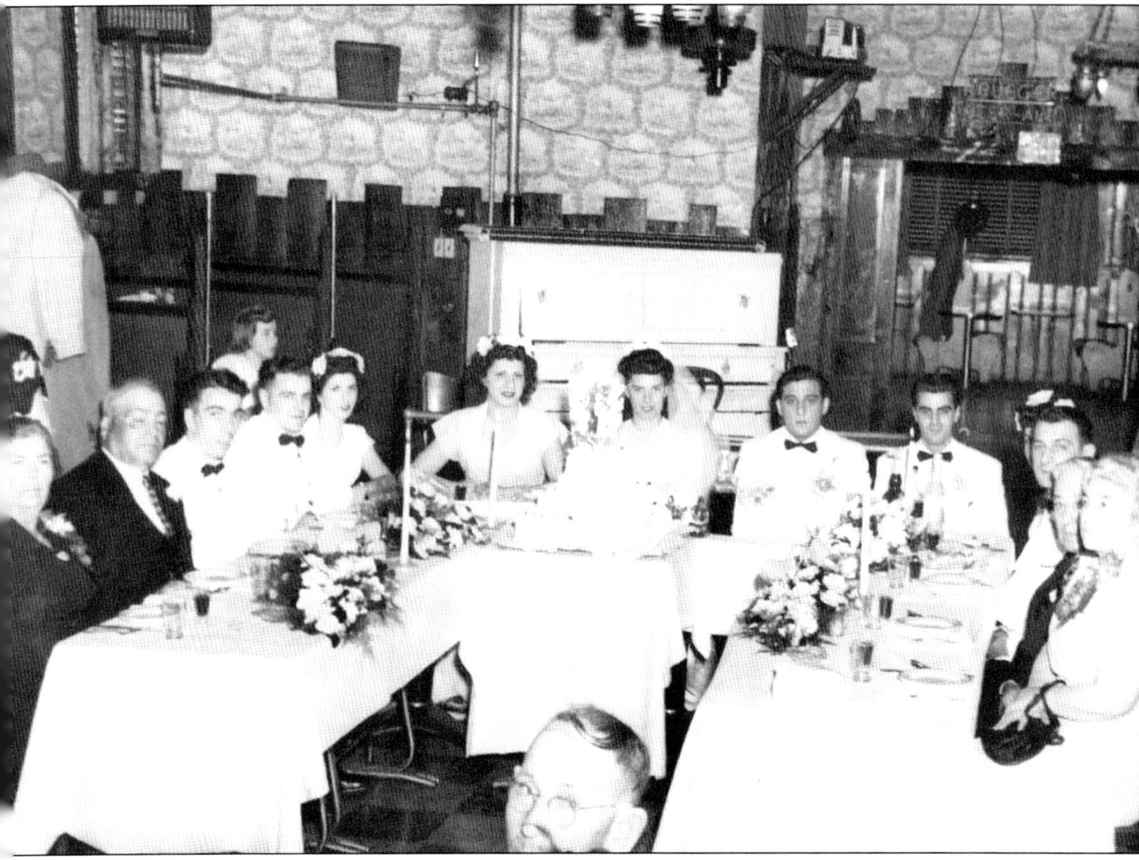

One of the "in" places to socialize at or have a function at the lake was Tilli's. This restaurant was located on North Quinsigamond Avenue, just north of the turnpike. Not only was it possible to get a meal or a drink at Tilli's, but the place also had candlepin bowling alleys in the basement! In this photograph we see one of the many weddings that was held at this popular spot. On May 22, 1948, Victor Mercadante and Rose Perna were married in St. Anne's Church and they are shown here at the head table during their wedding reception. Tilli's was still in business into the 1960s, until a 1965 fire totally destroyed the structure. The blaze was fueled by 75 dozen candles in glass holders that were stored in the building's basement. The property was eventually sold, and a fast-food restaurant was erected on this corner.